SECOND EDITION

SCHEDULING FOR BUILDERS

JERRY HOUSEHOLDER

Home Builder Press®
National Association of Home Builders
15th and M Streets, NW
Washington, DC 20005

Scheduling for Builders, second edition
ISBN 0-86718-353-5

© 1987, 1990 by Home Builder Press® of the National Association of Home Builders of the United States of America

All rights reserved. No part of this book may be reproduced or utilized in any form or by any means, electronic or mechanical, including photocopying and recording, or by any information storage and retrieval system without permission in writing from the publisher.

Printed in the United States of America

Library of Congress Cataloging-in-Publication Data

Householder, Jerry.
    Scheduling for builders / Jerry Householder. — 2nd ed.
      p. cm.
    ISBN 0-86718-353-5
    1. Construction industry—Management. 2. Scheduling (Management)
I. Title.
TH438.4.H68   1990
690'.068'5—dc20
                                                                                            90-47044
                                                                                               CIP

For further information, please contact—

Home Builder Press®
National Association of Home Builders
15th and M Streets, NW
Washington, DC 20005
(800) 223-2665

12/90 Merry-Orgel/Patterson 3M
7/93   McN&G Reprint 800

Contents

About the Author	vii
Acknowledgments	ix

Introduction — 1
Formal Planning Techniques — 2

Chapter 1   The Bar Chart — 5
Defining Activities — 5
Listing Activities — 6
Using the Bar Chart — 7

Chapter 2   The Planning Phase — 11
The Arrow Diagram — 11
The Precedence Network — 42
Helpful Tips — 54

Chapter 3   The Scheduling Phase — 55
Activity Duration — 56
Time Computations — 57
The Critical Path — 62
Float — 62
Rough-in Phase, House No. 2 — 64
Trim-out Phase, House No. 2 — 65
Long-Term Scheduling — 68
Contingencies — 68
Planning for Unusual Circumstances — 68

Chapter 4   The Monitoring Phase — 71
Short-Term Control — 71
Revising CPM Diagrams — 73
Crashing a Project — 75
Cost Forecasting — 76
Legal Implications — 81
Multiproject Scheduling — 81
Summary — 83

Figures

Figure 1 Bar Chart for House No. 1 — 8
Figure 2 Arrow Diagram for House No. 1 — 16
Figure 3 Arrow Diagram for Slab Phase, House No. 2 — 19
Figure 4 Arrow Diagram for Partial Rough-in Phase, House No. 2 — 27
Figure 5 Arrow Diagram for Partial Rough-in Phase, House No. 2 — 28
Figure 6 Arrow Diagram for Partial Rough-in Phase, House No. 2 — 29
Figure 7 Arrow Diagram for Complete Rough-in Phase, House No. 2 — 30
Figure 8 Arrow Diagram for Partial Trim-out Phase, House No. 2 — 34
Figure 9 Arrow Diagram for Partial Trim-out Phase, House No. 2 — 36
Figure 10 Arrow Diagram for Partial Trim-out Phase, House No. 2 — 37
Figure 11 Arrow Diagram for Partial Trim-out Phase, House No. 2 — 38
Figure 12a Complete Arrow Diagram, House No. 2 — 39
Figure 12b Complete Arrow Diagram, House No. 2 — 40
Figure 12c Complete Arrow Diagram, House No. 2 — 41
Figure 13a Precedence Network, House No. 1 — 45
Figure 13b Precedence Network, House No. 1 — 46
Figure 14a Precedence Network for Slab Phase, House No. 2 — 47
Figure 14b Precedence Network for Slab Phase, House No. 2 — 48
Figure 15 Precedence Network for Rough-in Phase, House No. 2 — 49
Figure 16 Precedence Network for Trim-out Phase, House No. 2 — 50
Figure 17 Arrow Diagram for Slab Phase, Drawn to a Time Scale, House No. 2 — 60
Figure 18 Arrow Diagram for Rough-in Phase, Drawn to a Time Scale, House No. 2 — 66
Figure 19 Arrow Diagram for Trim-out Phase, Drawn to a Time Scale, House No. 2 — 67
Figure 20 Using the Arrow Diagram for Short-Term Control — 72
Figure 21 Arrow Diagram with Long Flags — 74
Figure 22a Cash Flow Forecast, House No. 1 — 79
Figure 22b Cash Flow Forecast, House No. 1 — 80

About the Author

Jerry Householder, builder, professor, and author, has many years of experience as a general contractor. He has built over $100 million worth of residential, commercial, and industrial projects throughout the southeastern United States.

Currently the Director of Graduate Studies in Construction Management in the College of Architecture and Urban Studies at Virginia Polytechnic Institute and State University, Dr. Householder teaches courses in planning and scheduling, construction management, and construction law. A professor for ten years, the author holds a Ph.D. in civil engineering from the Georgia Institute of Technology.

Jerry Householder has coauthored NAHB's *Basic Construction Management: The Superintendent's Job* and been published in the *ASCE Journal of Construction Engineering and Management, The Arbitration Journal, Construction Management World,* and other periodicals. Dr. Householder has also held seminars on building topics at the NAHB Annual Convention.

Acknowledgments

This book was produced under the general direction of Kent Colton, NAHB Executive Vice President, in association with NAHB staff members James E. Johnson, Jr., Staff Vice President, Operations and Information Services; Adrienne Ash, Assistant Staff Vice President, Publishing Services; Rosanne O'Connor, Director of Publications and Project Editor; and David Rhodes, Art Director.

Special thanks go to Scott Hanks, Leon Rogers, and Jay Newitt for their careful review of the previous edition and manuscript. Thanks are also extended to the Business Management Committee of NAHB, to Sonia Wilder of the NAHB Business Management Department, and to Paul Sharp of Home Builders Institute.

Introduction

When formal scheduling methods were first developed, they were hailed as a major breakthrough for the construction industry. In fact, they are widely used today in heavy commercial and industrial construction. Yet despite proof of their usefulness, many home builders have not taken advantage of this managerial tool. The lack of widespread use does not mean that scheduling methods do not measure up to their reputation. Instead, the problem is that builders often have not put forth the effort necessary to understand how to use these methods.

Scheduling techniques require much effort to fully understand. This manual presents easy-to-understand, step-by-step procedures to help home builders control their work better. The reader must carefully study the principles outlined here, and like building a home, thoroughly complete and understand each part before going on to the next section.

Although every builder plans his or her work, most builders keep this plan or schedule in their heads. In the same way that the written word preserves, organizes, and details a person's thoughts, the schedule defines a construction plan. If a builder can think of a plan for organizing activities for a particular project, he or she can put this plan down on paper. Often, only then will ways to improve the plan become evident.

In essence, a critical path method (CPM) diagram is an organized schedule for the execution of a project.

Good business managers often list things to do, mark off completed tasks, and add new ones as they come up. This procedure helps these managers to become more efficient. A schedule is somewhat like a list of things to do except it goes one step further. It shows a flow diagram of when the things on the list must be done with respect to other things on the list.

To build a house without a set of prints would be difficult. Just as a good set of prints acts as a guide for building a house, a well-thought-out schedule acts as a guide for organizing and controlling the construction process.

In general, builders have always taken pride in their work. In the past, builders were considered more craftspeople than businesspeople. But a builder who is to prosper in today's competitive housing market must use the best managerial techniques available.

Many factors influence a home builder's success or failure. The mortgage interest rate, the strength of the local economy, and other factors over which the builder has no control affect profits. Therefore, the builder must do everything possible to manage work in a businesslike manner, and scheduling is the professional way to organize and control work.

Organization and control are the main benefits, but several other benefits can result from formal scheduling. For example, overhead is lower per house when building is faster. Home office expenses, such as rent, telephones, and office salaries, can be spread over more units.

Builders will pay less interest on construction money when the construction time is shorter. If the contractor is financing the construction or using borrowed money, this savings directly adds to the profit. If the contractor is receiving progress payments from the owner, the contractor's reputation is enhanced when buyers consistently have lower construction interest payments than expected.

Contractors who formally schedule their jobs often enjoy improved relations with subcontractors, suppliers, and financial institutions, as well as owners. Subcontractors and others prefer to work with builders who are dependable. Scheduling helps builders to predict accurately when they will need subcontractors and materials. Subcontractors often give preference to a builder who they know works from a schedule.

Anything that a builder can do to help better control the work is worth trying. However, to schedule effectively, the builder must know the subject thoroughly. The methods presented in this book allow the builder to plan and schedule to any level of detail needed.

Many builders manage their businesses by reacting to one crisis after another. These so-called crisis managers spend their time "putting out fires." Builders who use scheduling techniques find that they control their work instead of their work controlling them.

Formal Planning Techniques

Contractors use different methods for putting their plans on paper. The most common procedures are developed in this book as follows:

- bar charts
- arrow diagrams
- precedence networks

The arrow diagrams and precedence networks are forms of critical path method scheduling, but bar charts are not. Therefore, the term CPM diagram can mean either an arrow diagram or a precedence network.

Furthermore, the implementation of these procedures consists of three phases:

- planning
- scheduling
- monitoring

The planning phase is the most important of the three. In this phase, the builder—

- lists the work necessary to complete the project
- determines the relationship of the activities to each other or which activities must be done before others start

Since the work to be done on a job usually varies from one job to another, the work sequence for any one job will be unique. Also, different builders will choose to build the same house differently. Therefore, the person responsible for building the project must contribute to the decisions during the planning phase. When the planning phase is logically presented in an arrow diagram or precedence network, the builder will have a complete layout of the way in which the facility will be constructed.

Many builders decide to stop with the planning phase when they find that their work proceeds much more easily. The scheduling phase, while considered by some as less important than the planning phase, is still quite valuable. Scheduling sets time limits for each planned activity and allows the contractor to predict when different parts of the work will begin and end.

As the project proceeds, builders should periodically review and compare its status to the plan sequence. Builders can change the schedule and even the sequence of activities to reflect new conditions. Seldom does a project go exactly as planned. A late delivery or an absent subcontractor requires midcourse corrections in the schedule and sometimes in the planned sequence of activities.

The following chapters discuss each of these phases. The first chapter describes how to draw bar charts. The second chapter explains the planning phase with techniques on drawing arrow diagrams and precedence networks.

The third chapter covers the scheduling phase. The builder will learn how to forecast the time a job needs and how to plan work for both the short and long term.

The fourth chapter details the monitoring phase with techniques on using schedules to help with short-term control and changing schedules to deal with unforeseen contingencies. For short-term use, the schedule can help to ensure the timely delivery of materials and to coordinate subcontractors. Unique ways to track the progress of a job are demonstrated. Finally, the builder will learn how to tie costs to the schedule to create cash flow forecasts and how to manage multiproject schedules.

The beginner can use the scheduling techniques explained in this book a little at a time. A bar chart or simple logic diagram without time values can be used at first. Then, as skills improve, more intricate aspects can be added.

CHAPTER 1

The Bar Chart

The builder or superintendent must study the plans and specifications carefully before drawing a bar chart, arrow diagram, or precedence network. As mentioned previously, the person actually in charge of running the job in the field must be involved in drawing the diagram or otherwise it will be useless. Generally, when planning a project, most builders review the job in their heads and write down the step-by-step activities as if they were actually building the job.

Defining Activities

Whether the plan is to appear on a bar chart or CPM diagram, the builder should begin by breaking the project down into practical phases such as—

- slab and foundation
- rough-in
- trim-out

The builder then breaks down each phase even further. Knowing how far to break down the activities is a matter of individual preference, but here is a secret to how detailed the activities list should be. The list should be detailed enough to help the builder manage activities but not so much as to become cumbersome. A good rule is to separate activities by subcontractor or individual activity of a subcontractor. After building a few homes using formal planning methods, most builders can adjust the level of detail to suit their own individual needs.

Some materials require a long lead time for delivery. The plan should indicate such items as separate activities. For example, in some areas, roof trusses or brick must be ordered on the day the field work starts or even before.

Two case studies will be used throughout this book to demonstrate how to plan and schedule a job. The first example, called House No. 1, is a simple house with few tasks. The second example, called House No. 2, has a little greater detail.

House No. 1 has the following general specifications:

- one-story house—approximately 1,200 square feet
- slab on grade with monolithic footings
- truss roof
- brick veneer
- drywall throughout with stained trim
- vinyl floor throughout
- ceramic tile around tub
- landscaped yard
- asphalt drive
- central heat
- slide-in range with no other appliances
- insulated walls and ceilings
- standard roofing, electrical work, and plumbing
- slab, rough-in, and final inspections
- no garage

The activities list for House No. 1 will include—

- administrative tasks, such as obtaining permits
- deliveries of material, such as framing materials and drywall
- actual work activities, such as grading the lot and framing

Listing Activities

Work should flow without interruption. Two or more distinct parts of a particular task occurring at different times in the job need to be scheduled as separate activities. For example, the electrical work should be divided into electrical rough-in and electrical trim-out.

Here is a list of 36 activities for building House No. 1:

1. Get permit.
2. Grade lot.
3. Get temporary power.
4. Get water to site.
5. Deliver brick, mortar mix, and sand.
6. Form, plumb, wrap, and inspect slab.
7. Pour slab.
8. Deliver framing materials.
9. Frame.

10. Deliver roofing.
11. Put roofing on.
12. Rough in electrical work.
13. Rough in heating, ventilating, and air conditioning (HVAC).
14. Top out plumbing.
15. Brick exterior.
16. Insulate walls.
17. Clean before rough-in inspection.
18. Do rough-in inspection.
19. Install septic system or hook up sewer.
20. Deliver drywall.
21. Hang and finish drywall.
22. Clean drywall scraps.
23. Put down vinyl floor.
24. Deliver trim.
25. Stain trim and paint interior.
26. Install cabinets.
27. Install wood trim.
28. Install ceramic tile.
29. Trim out plumbing.
30. Trim out electrical work.
31. Trim out HVAC.
32. Paint exterior.
33. Insulate attic.
34. Do final clean.
35. Landscape and pave driveway.
36. Do final inspection.

Using the Bar Chart

A bar chart is simply a listing of the activities necessary to build the job with a bar drawn on a calendar showing when each activity occurs. Therefore, drawing a bar chart requires a time estimate of each activity.

This most familiar and easily understood form of scheduling is an easy way to project a schedule for a construction job. Figure 1 shows a bar chart

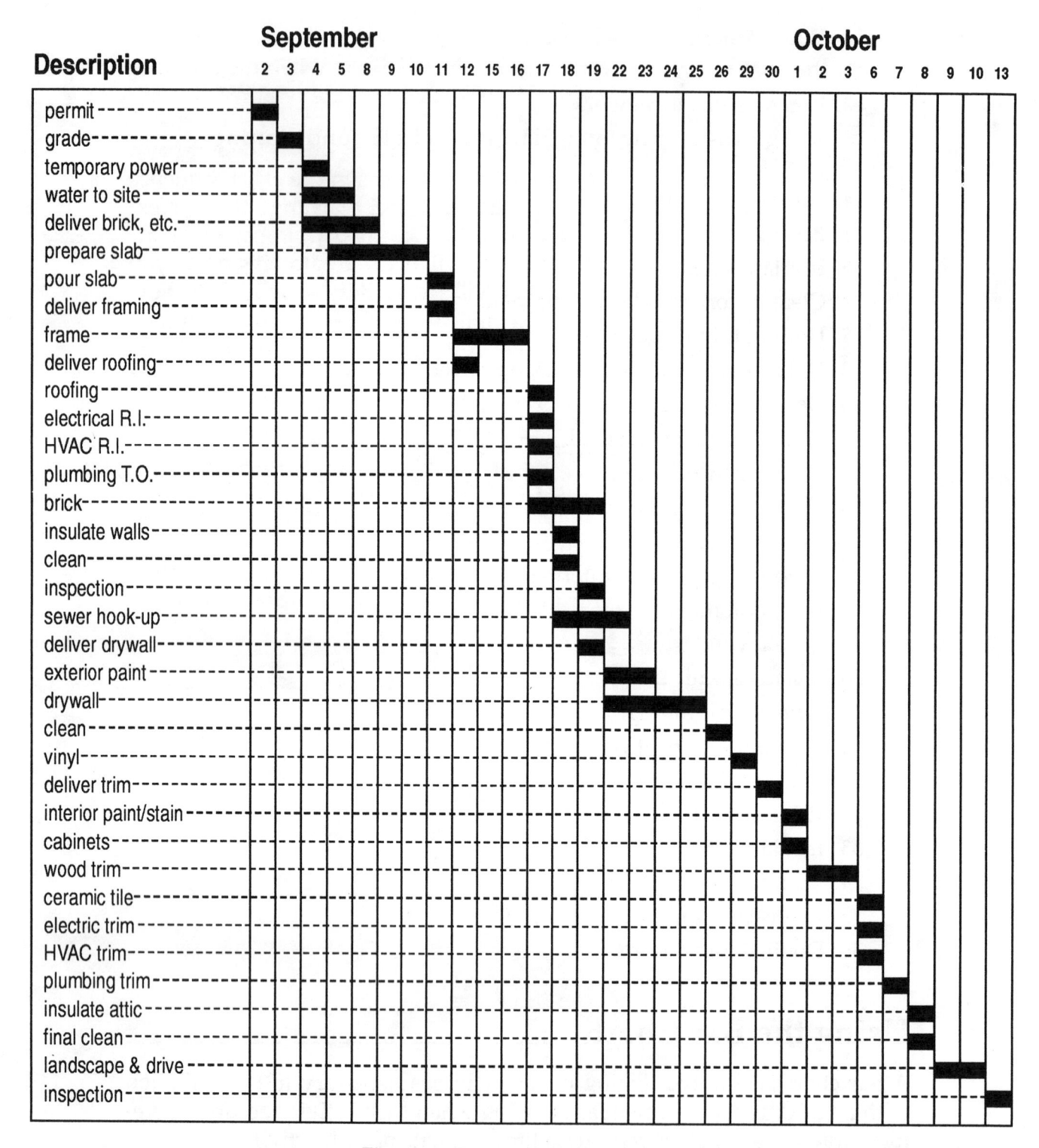

Figure 1 Bar Chart for House No. 1

8 Scheduling for Builders

for the complete list of 36 activities with projected time slots for House No. 1. The bars on the calendar portion of the chart indicate when the activities are to occur. According to this chart, 30 working days are required to complete the house.

To draw the bar chart, you first list the activities down the left-hand side of the page. It is unnecessary to list the activities in the exact sequence in which they occur. You can always go back and rearrange them. Next draw vertical lines showing all the work days. Draw a bar opposite each activity to show when you think that activity will occur. In drawing a bar, you must answer two questions: (1) When will the activity start and (2) how long will it last? In determining when an activity will start, you must look at the other activities that affect the one you are drawing. A more detailed discussion of determining how long an activity lasts is given later in the book, so for now experience is the best guide.

One of the biggest advantages of the bar chart is its simple visual presentation. It clearly shows when an activity will start and end, so managers and workers can understand at a glance how the work will progress.

The strengths of the bar chart can also become weaknesses. The bar chart cannot show the complex interdependence between the various activities. Therefore, the bar chart is best used as a general planning and communication tool where a graphic display of the interrelationships is unnecessary.

CHAPTER 2

The Planning Phase

During the planning phase, the builder decides how to build the project. This chapter explains how to draw arrow diagrams and precedence networks. The construction of an arrow diagram or precedence network is a form of planning because these diagrams show the plan or logic of how the different activities depend on one another. In this chapter, the diagrams will not show when the activities are scheduled to be done except as they relate to each other. The process of determining when the activities occur on a calendar is called scheduling and is explained in Chapter 3.

Network logic shows the relationships between activities where a bar chart does not. For example, Figure 1 shows that the drywall will be delivered on September 19 and that the hanging and finishing will begin the next working day on September 22. What Figure 1 does *not* show is that the delivery *must* come before the hanging. The bar chart also shows that painting the exterior starts on September 22, which has nothing to do with the drywall delivery. These relationships among drywall delivery, hanging and finishing, and painting the exterior are obvious. Relationships between other activities are not always so easy to see. A CPM diagram that shows what activities must be finished before another activity can begin is much more informative than a bar chart.

The Arrow Diagram

In this book the arrow diagram will be used to show how CPM diagrams are drawn because it is easier to draw than a precedence network. However, precedence networks are usually more easily understood than arrow diagrams, especially by those unfamiliar with CPM diagrams. Likewise, precedence networks are commonly used as computer output and, therefore, will be fully shown at the end of this chapter.

On an arrow diagram, an arrow represents an activity. The name of the activity is written above the arrow.

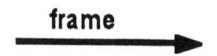

$$\xrightarrow{\text{frame}}$$

A circle in an arrow diagram represents a point in time or an event. The number in the circle is used for identification and is called the event number. An event is a point in time. Sometimes the circle is called a node instead of an event.

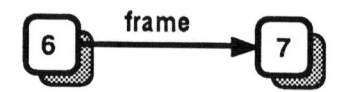

$$\boxed{6} \xrightarrow{\text{frame}} \boxed{7}$$

For example, when the slab has been finished and the lumber delivered, the framing is ready to start. On this diagram, that point in time is called event 6, and when the framing is finished is called event 7. The beginning event of an activity is called its "i" and the ending event is called its "j." In this example, the "i" for framing is 6 and the "j" for framing is 7, so framing may be referred to as activity 6-7. The event numbers themselves have no special significance other than to give a name to that particular activity. The only reason that numbers are used in naming events is so the arrow diagram can be put on a computer. In other words, if a computer is not used, the numbers are not needed. Many people unfamiliar with the arrow diagram will try to make something more than is intended out of the event numbers.

The next principle about arrow diagrams is that arrows can line up. When an arrow starts at a circle where another arrow ends, the first activity must be completed before proceeding to the next activity. In this example, the slab must be poured before the framing can start.

$$\boxed{5} \xrightarrow{\text{pour slab}} \boxed{6} \xrightarrow{\text{frame}} \boxed{7}$$

If more than one activity is shown going into a circle, they must all be complete before the next activity can start. This figure shows that the framing cannot start until both framing delivery and pouring the slab are done.

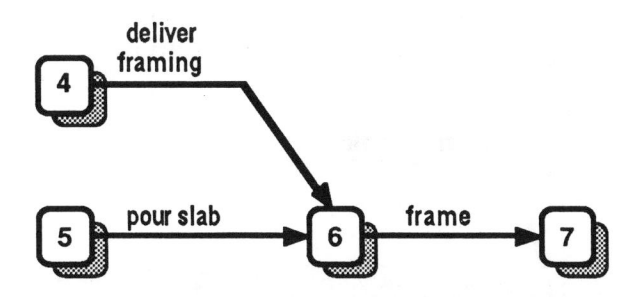

The delivery of framing material and pouring the slab constrain the start of framing and are therefore called constraints.

In arrow diagrams, each activity is subject to the following questions:

1. What activities must precede this activity? Most activities have a logical sequence that dictates when they can begin. The slab must be poured and the framing material delivered before the framing begins.
2. What activities cannot start until this activity has been completed? Plumbing top-out, HVAC rough-in, electrical rough-in, brick work, and roofing cannot start until the framing is finished.
3. What activities can occur at the same time as this activity? While the framing is going on in this example, the roofing, brick, mortar mix, and sand can be delivered, and the water may be brought to the job either by hooking on to existing lines or drilling a well. One of the keys to effective planning is to have simultaneous activities whenever possible.

Constraints

Constraints for the start of each activity may be classified as hard or soft constraints. Some activities absolutely cannot be started until others are complete. Such constraints are termed hard constraints. For example, a house cannot be roofed until the roof deck is on. A builder may decide that a certain activity should be complete before starting another activity. This plan is not absolutely necessary but is more for convenience. For example, a contractor may decide that he or she will not install the vinyl floor covering until the painting is done. When this type of logic is used, this is a soft constraint.

Another principle about these diagrams is that no two activities can have the same beginning and ending designation or i-j number. Two activities that start and end together must use a special dummy arrow. After the walls are insulated on House No. 1, two activities can happen—the rough-in inspection and the drywall delivery. After these two activities are complete, the drywall may be hung. This relationship may be shown as follows:

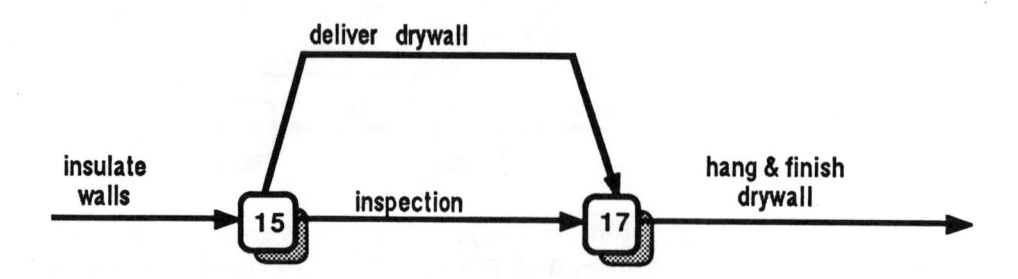

This diagram, however, violates the principle of the same i-j numbers because both the inspection and drywall delivery would be activity 15-17. The following diagram shows the correct way to represent these activities.

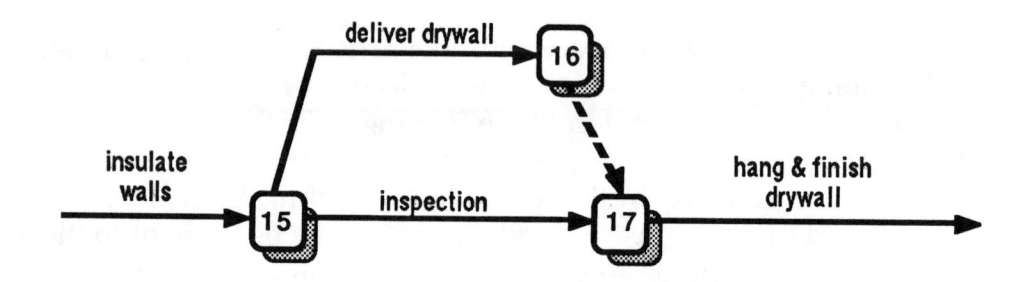

By inserting a new event circle or node, number 16, and drawing a dashed dummy arrow from 16 to 17, the rule is satisfied. The inspection is activity 15-17 and the drywall delivery is activity 15-16. A dummy arrow shows relationships and takes no time.

Another use of the dummy arrow can be seen when two activities occur simultaneously followed by two more simultaneous activities.

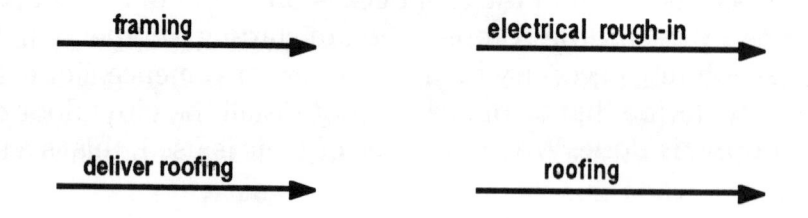

14 Scheduling for Builders

One event circle connecting the four activities would look like this:

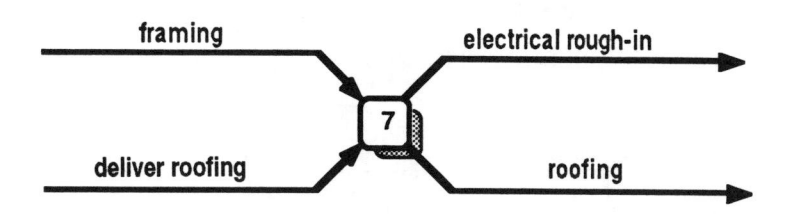

This diagram indicates that the electrical rough-in cannot start until the framing is done, which is correct. Also, the roofing cannot start until the framing is done and the roofing material delivered. However, this diagram also indicates that the electrical rough-in cannot start until the roofing is delivered, which is incorrect. The electrical rough-in can be shown to be independent of the roofing delivery as follows:

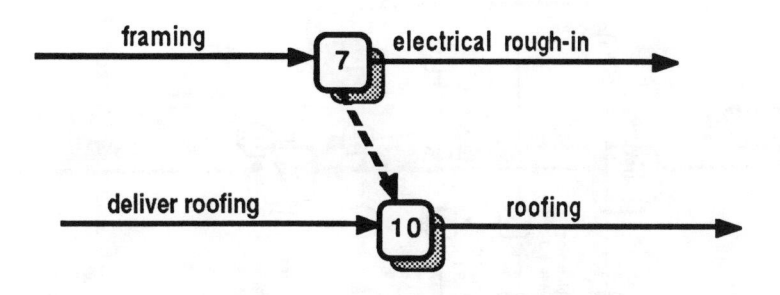

This configuration with the dummy arrow indicates that the roofing depends on both the framing and roofing delivery, but the electrical rough-in depends only on the framing.

Compare the complete arrow diagram for House No. 1 as shown in Figure 2 with the bar chart in Figure 1.

Notice first that the arrow diagram shows what activities must be done before others can start. In other words, it shows the interrelationships between all the activities. Study the diagram carefully and try to understand the logic shown. Be aware that there are many ways to organize the work for a particular job and this diagram shows just one way.

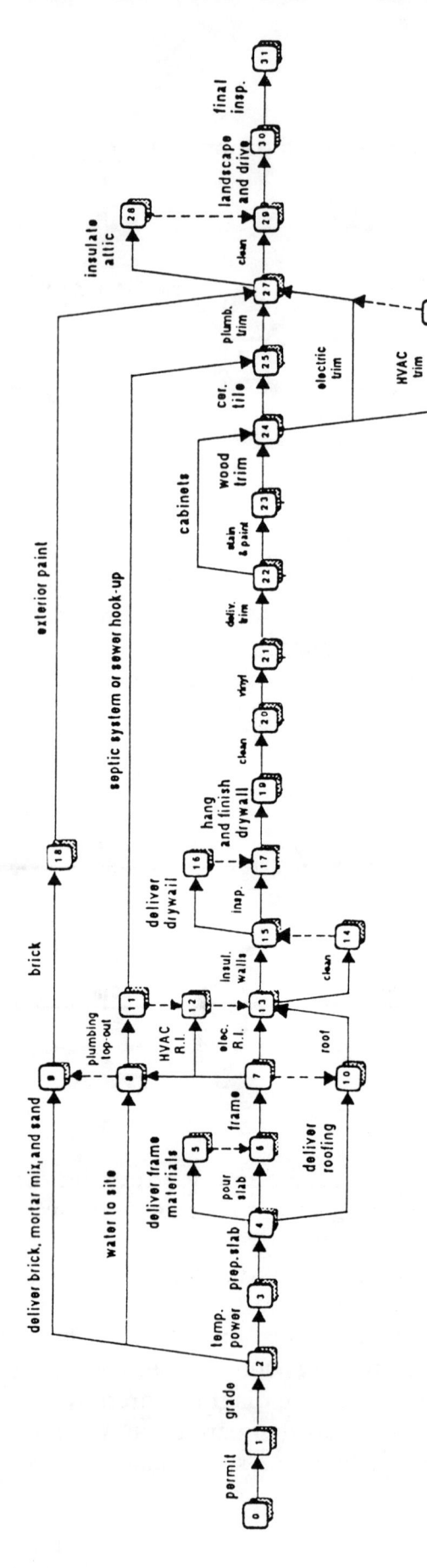

Figure 2 Arrow Diagram for House No. 1

16 Scheduling for Builders

Second, notice that the arrow diagram does not show when the activities occur or how long they last like the bar chart does. This arrow diagram can be drawn to a time scale, and you will learn how to do so in Chapter 3.

Planning the Slab Phase for House No. 2

An arrow diagram for House No. 2 will now be developed in more detail than for House No. 1. House No. 2 has the following general specifications:

- one-story house—approximately 1,800 square feet
- slab on grade formed by concrete blocks as shown below
- garage slab four inches down separated from house by permanent pressure-treated 2x6s as shown below

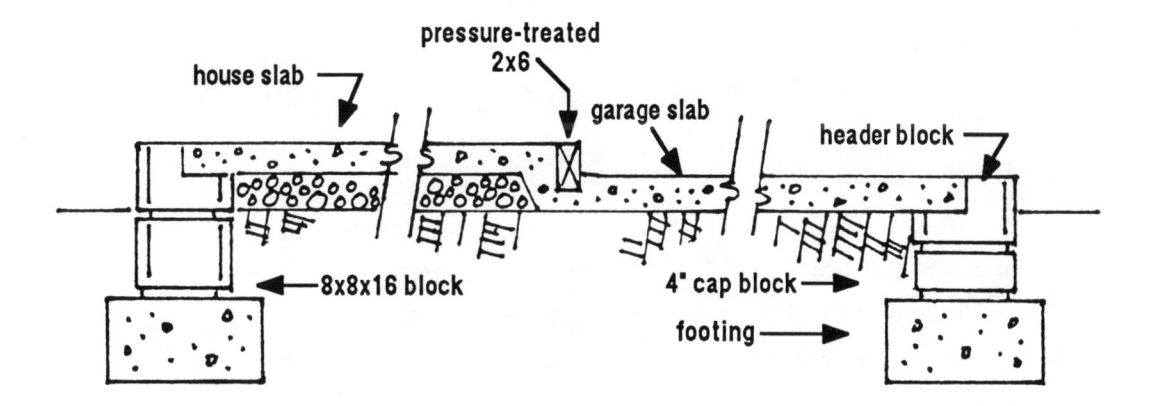

- truss roof
- exterior siding
- drywall throughout with painted trim
- vinyl floor in kitchen and baths
- carpet
- prefabricated fireplace with wood chimney outside
- masonry hearth and interior masonry face
- fiberglass one-piece tubs
- garage door
- gutters
- landscaped yard
- concrete drive
- central heating and air conditioning
- slide-in range and dishwasher
- insulated walls and ceilings
- standard roofing, electrical work, and plumbing

Here is a list of 24 activities for preparing the lot and pouring the slab for House No. 2:

1. Obtain permit.
2. Establish house location.
3. Grade lot.
4. Lay out footings.
5. Dig footings.
6. Set grade stakes in footing trench.
7. Get footing inspection.
8. Pour footings.
9. Set batter boards.
10. Deliver header blocks, mortar mix, and sand.
11. Lay blocks.
12. Rough in underslab plumbing.
13. Deliver gravel.
14. Spread gravel.
15. Treat for termites.
16. Form garage.
17. Place welded wire mesh and polyethylene.
18. Get slab inspection.
19. Survey slab.
20. Pour slab.
21. Get water to site.
22. Set temporary power pole.
23. Have power brought to temporary pole.
24. Get builder's risk insurance.

One configuration of an arrow diagram for these activities is shown in Figure 3. This diagram tells the following:

1. The first thing that must be done is to get a building permit (0-1).
2. After the building permit is issued, the location of the house is established (1-2).
3. Next the lot is graded and the house location leveled (2-3).

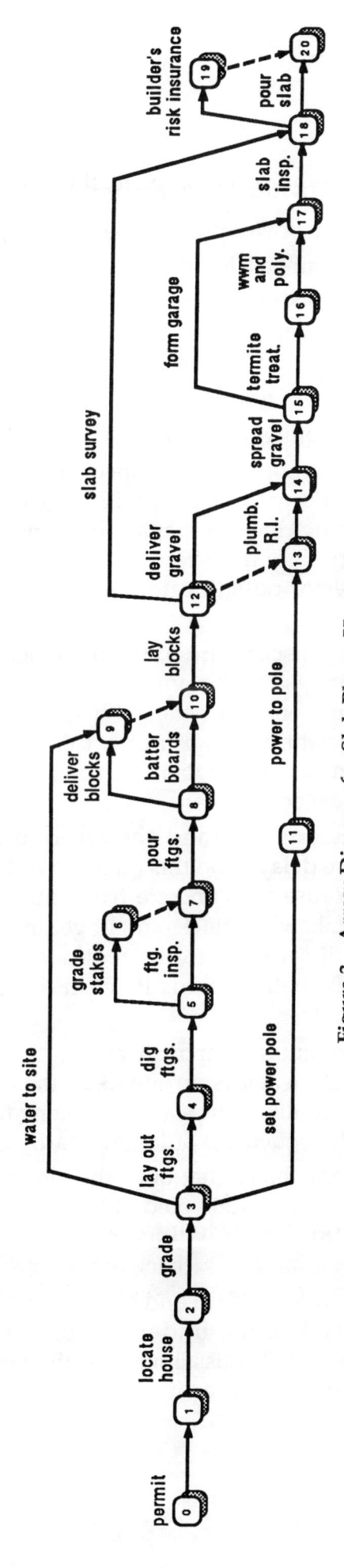

Figure 3 Arrow Diagram for Slab Phase, House No. 2

4. Once the rough grading is complete, three things can start:

   a. The temporary power pole can be set (3-11).
   b. The footings can be laid out (3-4).
   c. Water can be brought to the site (3-9). Usually this means that a water meter is set and a faucet attached. Activity 3-9 should be complete before the masons are ready to lay blocks.

5. As soon as the footings are laid out, they can be dug (4-5).

6. The diagram indicates that an inspection of the footings is required (5-7) and grade stakes will be driven in the bottom of the footing ditch to prepare it for pouring the concrete (5-6). Also, since the activities are simultaneous, obviously the inspector doesn't care whether the grade stakes are in place.

7. After the footing inspection and the placement of the grade stakes, the footings can be poured (7-8). These diagrams should have only enough detail to help builders organize their work efficiently. For example, this diagram doesn't show but assumes that the footings will have enough time to set before the blocks are laid.

8. The block delivery (8-9) and the erection of the batter boards (8-10) are delayed on this diagram until the footings are poured because the concrete truck might disturb the batter boards. Likewise, blocks might get in the way of the concrete truck if set close to the footings and hinder the placement of the batter boards if set in the middle of the house area.

9. After the blocks are delivered (8-9), the batter boards are up (8-10), and the water is on site (3-9), the blocks may be laid (10-12). Naturally, if the slab were being formed differently, this whole sequence would necessarily change.

10. Next the diagram shows that once the blocks are laid (10-12), the gravel may be delivered (12-14) and the slab survey done (12-18), which will assure the lender that the house will meet minimum setback requirements.

11. Also after the blocks are laid and the power to service pole is complete (11-13), the underslab plumbing may be roughed in (13-14). This assumes that the plumber wants power to help in cutting the pipe.

12. Spreading the gravel (14-15) may start when the gravel is delivered and the plumbing rough-in is complete, including a plumbing inspection if necessary.
13. After the gravel has been spread, the slab may be treated for termites (15-16).
14. Also after the gravel is spread, the garage may be formed (15-17). This activity also includes forming the garage door opening.
15. After the termite treatment, the polyethylene and welded wire mesh are placed (16-17).
16. In this example, a slab inspection is required (17-18).
17. Once the slab has passed inspection and the survey is complete, the slab may be poured (18-20). It is a good idea to make sure the slab survey is done before pouring because mistakes in layout sometimes occur. And the more that is in place, the more difficult it is to correct mistakes.
18. Notice that the builder's risk insurance is taken out at this time (18-19). The builder's risk insurance should be in place before framing is started. Some lenders require it earlier. If your lender doesn't, the only risk before this time is that of vandalism to the plumbing.

Planning the Rough-in Phase for House No. 2

To further illustrate the use of the arrow diagram, the rough-in phase—framing, heating, and plumbing—will now be developed for House No. 2. The first thing to do is to list all the activities this phase requires. The following list is just one way to break it down. (The first 24 activities were for pouring the slab.)

25. Deliver rough framing order, which includes lumber, roof decking, and the like.
26. Do rough framing, which includes walls, roof, and roof deck.
27. Deliver siding and cornice material.
28. Deliver prefabricated fireplace.
29. Deliver one-piece fiberglass bathtub units.
30. Finish framing to include sheathing, windows, and the like.
31. Set fireplace.

32. Run sewer and water lines to house.
33. Measure for and order sheet metal chimney cap supplied by heating and air conditioning subcontractor.
34. Install cornice (facia and soffit).
35. Install siding.
36. Install roofing.
37. Deliver garage door.
38. Top out plumbing—supply lines, drains, and vents.
39. Rough in HVAC.
40. Inspect plumbing.
41. Paint exterior.
42. Do electrical rough-in, which includes telephones.
43. Inspect electrical work.
44. Install gutters.
45. Insulate walls.
46. Conduct intermediate cleanup.
47. Do rough-in grading for driveway.
48. Form drive.
49. Pour concrete drive.
50. Deliver splash blocks for gutters and downspouts.
51. Inspect.
52. Stock sheetrock.
53. Landscape.

These activities may be organized in many ways. The following is just one way. What's important here is how the logic expresses the planner's ideas, not whether this is the best way to proceed for every given case.

After the slab is finished, two activities can start immediately—the sewer and water tie-in and the delivery of the rough framing order.

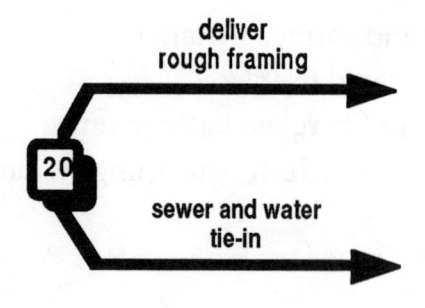

As soon as the rough framing is delivered, four activities can occur—rough framing, fireplace delivery, siding and cornice delivery, and bathtub delivery.

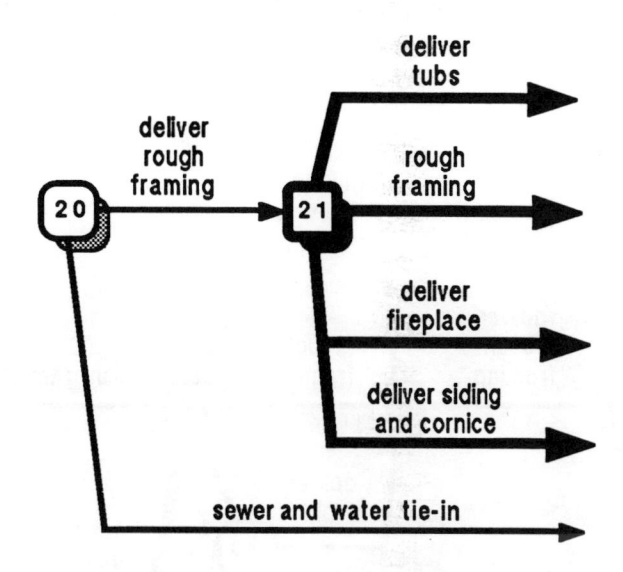

Before the finish framing is begun (sheathing and the like), the rough framing must be finished and the tubs and fireplace delivered.

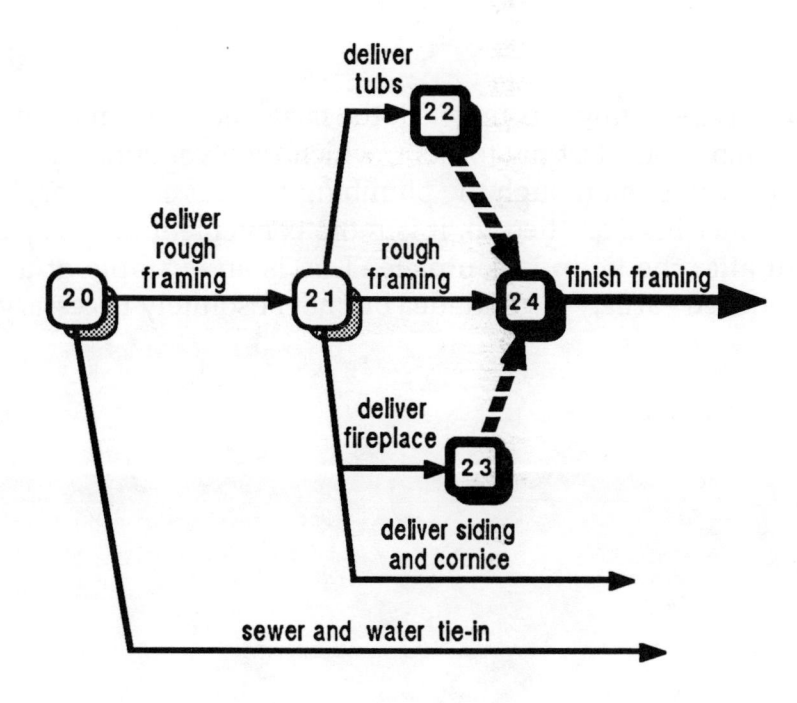

Chapter 2 The Planning Phase

The prefabricated fireplace is set while the finish framing is going on. As soon as the fireplace is set and the chimney framed and finished, the metal chimney cap can be ordered. In this case, the heating and air conditioning subcontractor is making the cap. The siding material, part of which will be used on the chimney on this house, must be on the chimney before the chimney cap is ordered.

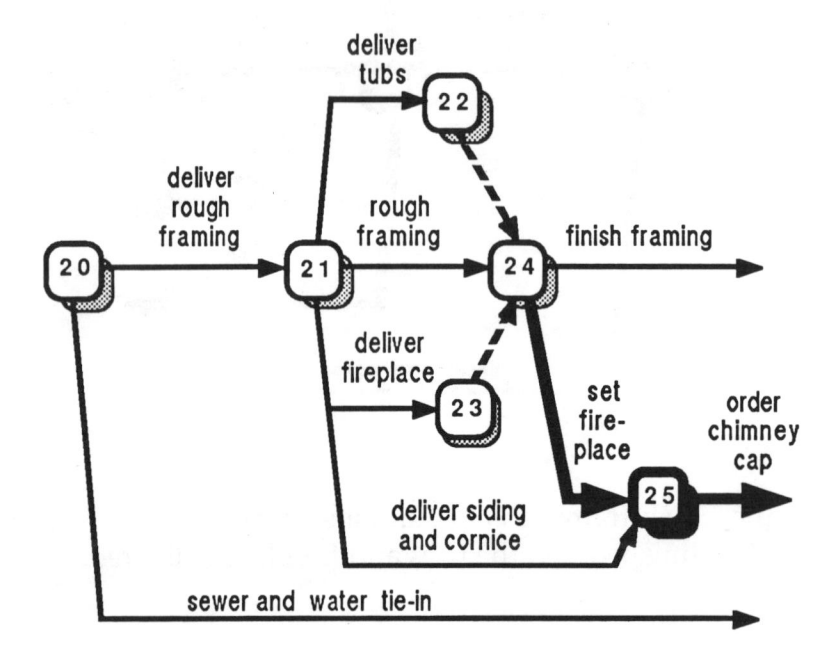

As soon as the framing is finished, the facia and soffit may be installed. Also the plumber can start the top-out, which involves running the supply, drains, and vents. Even though the plumbing top-out could start before the sewer and water lines are tied in, it is more convenient on this job to start the top-out after the tie-in is complete. This is an example of a soft constraint mentioned earlier—a good idea but not absolutely necessary.

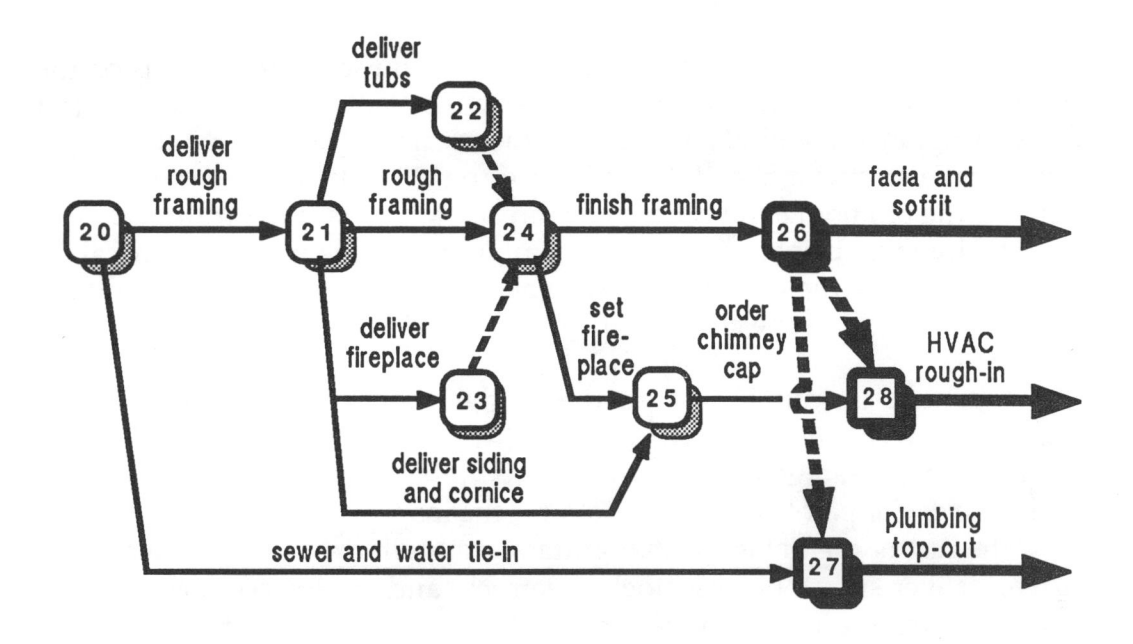

When the facia and soffit activity is complete, the roofing and siding may be installed and the garage door delivered. The garage door is delivered before time to hang it so that it can be painted without all its hardware. On this house, the painter would rather paint the garage door with the house exterior and then touch up the door after it is hung.

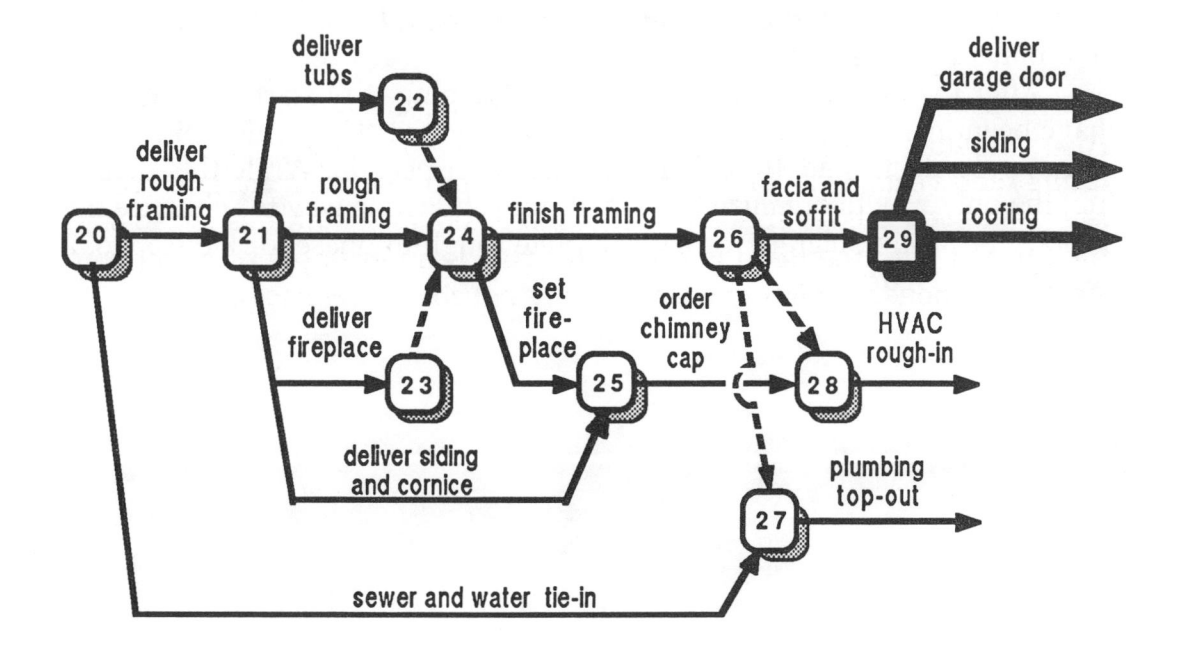

Chapter 2 The Planning Phase 25

After the roofing and siding are installed and the garage door is on the job, the exterior painting may be done. Also the electrical rough-in can start after the plumber and HVAC subcontractor are finished. The electrician might have started earlier, but the builder on this job felt that it would be better if the plumbing and ductwork were already in (see Figure 4).

A plumbing inspection follows the plumbing work and an electrical inspection follows the electrical work. These two inspections must be done and the roofing must be complete before the wall insulation is installed (see Figure 5).

A general cleanup is scheduled after the roofing. The rough-in inspection for the whole house is scheduled after the wall insulation and cleanup. Notice that the garage door delivery (29-30), the siding installation (29-32), and the exterior paint are not required for the inspection (see Figure 6).

The rest of the items—install gutters, rough in drive, form drive, pour drive, deliver splash blocks, stock sheetrock, and landscape—are also unnecessary for the rough-in inspection. They can be performed independently of the inspection. The gutters are installed after the painting is complete. The splash blocks are delivered while the gutters are being installed. This is another good example of a soft constraint. It is not always the best course of action to do an activity as soon as possible. The splash blocks could have been delivered much earlier, but delivery at this time is more convenient. The sheetrock may be delivered after the insulation and during the inspection. Pouring the drive follows forming the drive, which follows roughing in the drive. Roughing in the drive follows the plumbing inspection because the water and sewer ditches can be filled in at the same time and may even cross the drive.

After the driveway is poured, the landscaping may start if the gutters have been installed and the splash blocks delivered. The landscaping itself is not precedent to anything before the final inspection. While this plan is not the only way to organize this job, it does show one way to sequence the work. The arrow diagram for the complete rough-in phase for House No. 2 is shown in Figure 7.

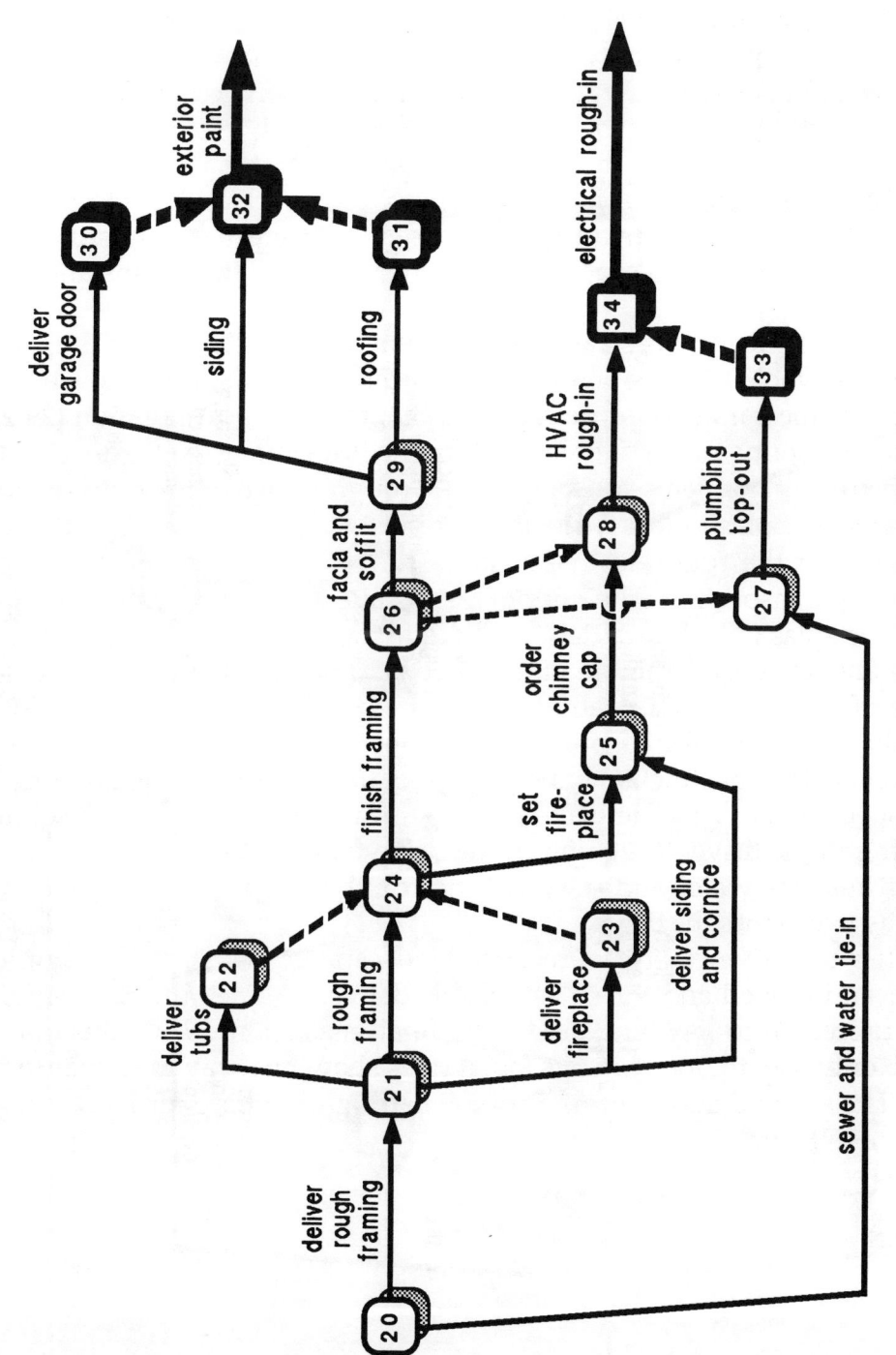

Figure 4   Arrow Diagram for Partial Rough-in Phase, House No. 2

Chapter 2 The Planning Phase   27

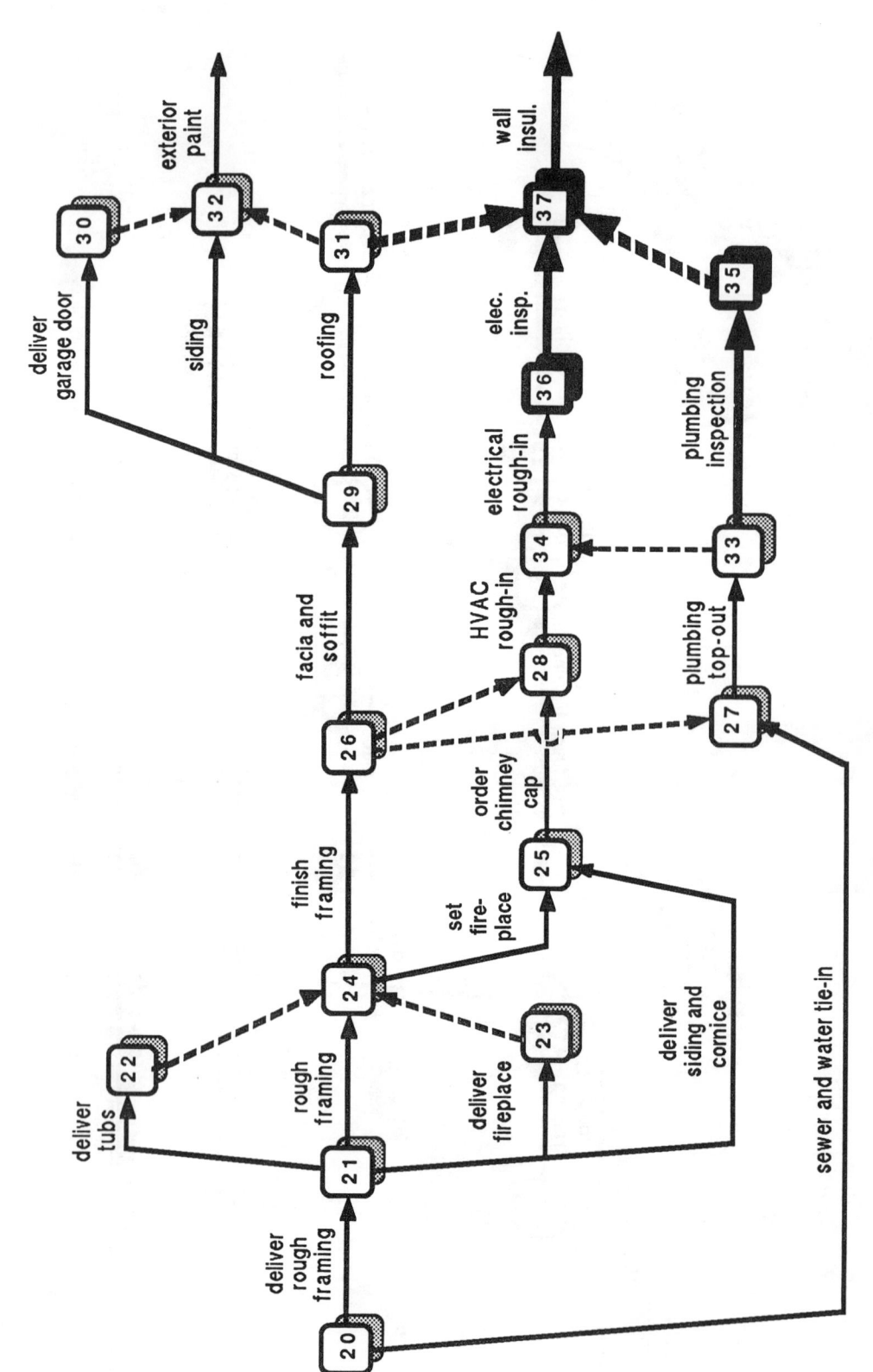

Figure 5   Arrow Diagram for Partial Rough-in Phase, House No. 2

28   Scheduling for Builders

Figure 6 Arrow Diagram for Partial Rough-in Phase, House No. 2

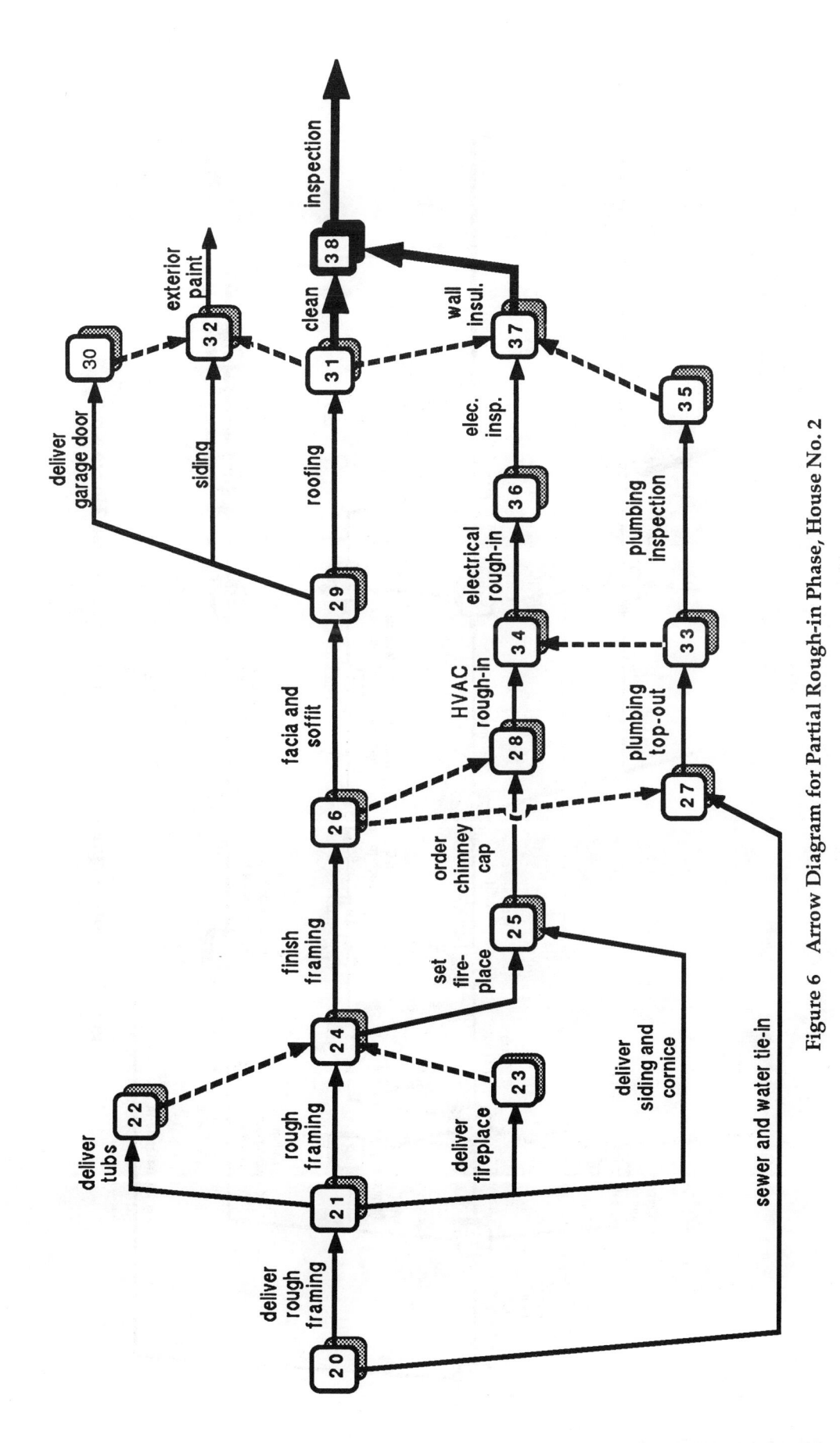

Chapter 2 The Planning Phase   29

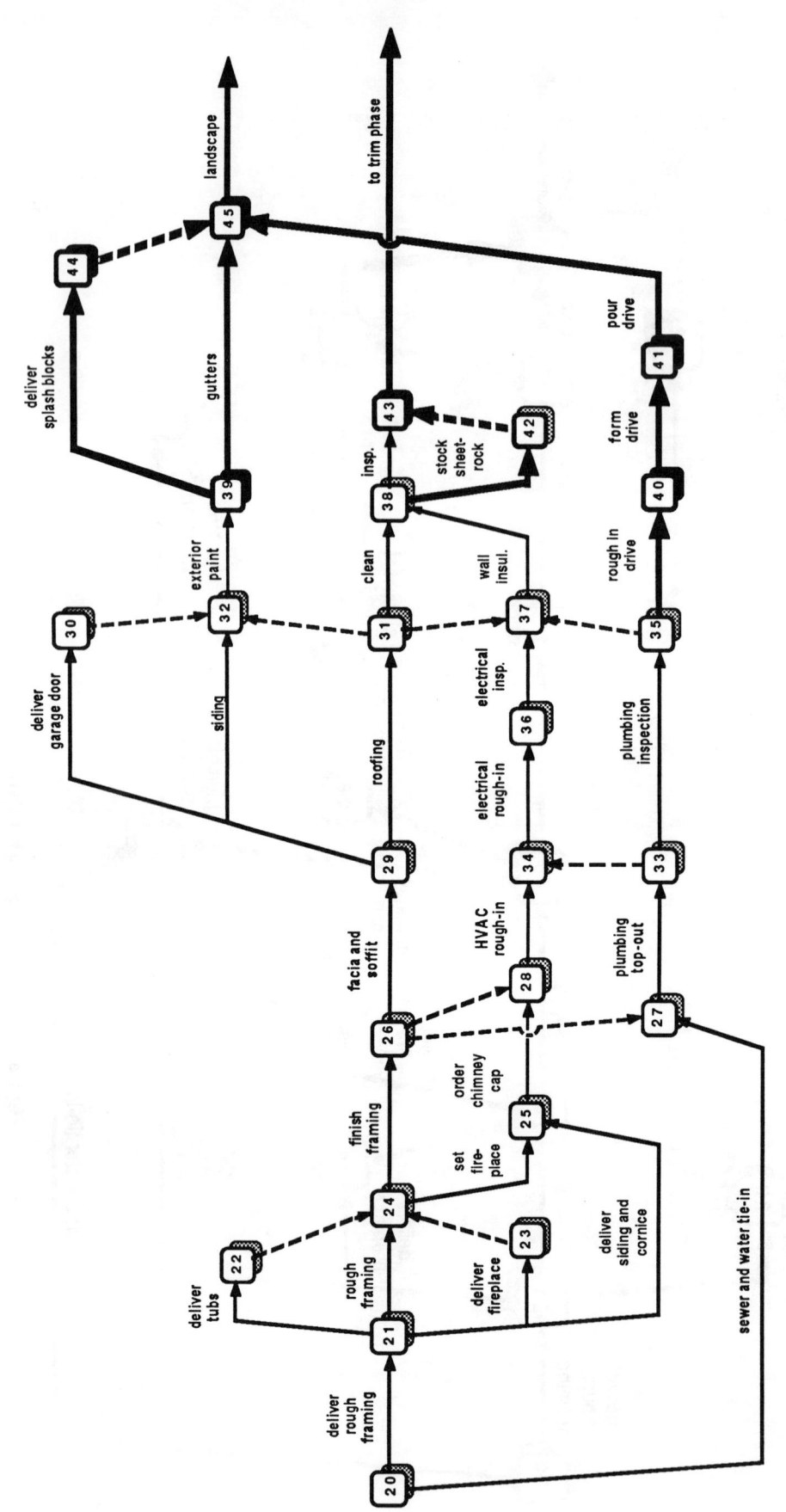

Figure 7 Arrow Diagram for Complete Rough-in Phase, House No. 2

30 Scheduling for Builders

Planning the Trim-out Phase for House No. 2

As in the rough-in phase, the first thing to do in the trim-out phase is to develop a list of activities:

54. Hang and finish sheetrock.
55. Clean up sheetrock trash.
56. Deliver wood trim.
57. Install interior wood trim except for base in vinyl areas.
58. Install garage door.
59. Paint interior.
60. Hang wallpaper in baths, entry, and kitchen.
61. Install vinyl.
62. Deliver cabinets, bathroom mirrors, and range hood.
63. Install cabinets, mirrors, range hood, base in vinyl areas, and hardware.
64. Deliver dishwasher and stove.
65. Install inside fireplace masonry.
66. Trim out HVAC.
67. Trim out plumbing.
68. Trim out electrical work.
69. Deliver lighting package.
70. Inspect electrical work.
71. Clean up.
72. Touch up paint.
73. Blow attic insulation.
74. Install carpet.
75. Conduct final inspection.

Starting with event 43, the sheetrock may be hung and finished.

hang and finish sheetrock
[43] →

It is best not to deliver the interior wood trim until after the sheetrock work is finished. The sheetrock scrap may be cleaned up then at the same time.

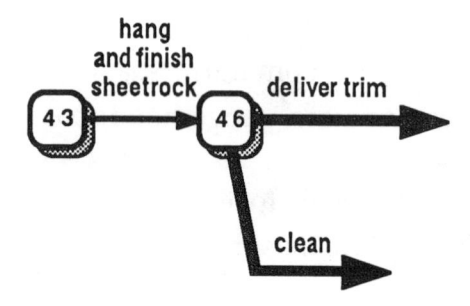

[43] **hang and finish sheetrock** → [46] **deliver trim** →
                                          clean →

After the trim is delivered and the sheetrock cleaned up, the interior wood trim can be installed. Assuming sheetrock is used in the garage, the garage door can now be hung.

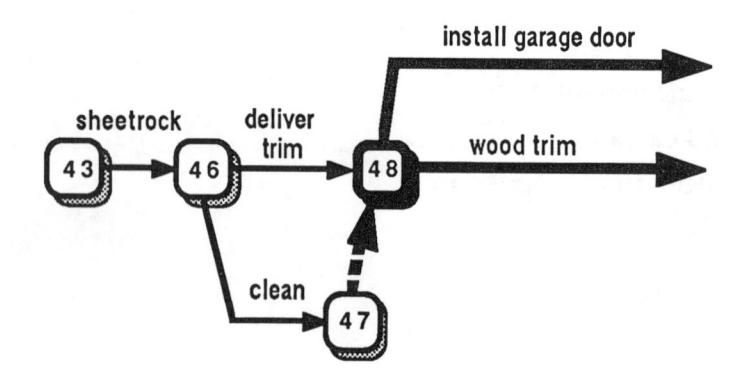

[43] **sheetrock** → [46] **deliver trim** → [48] **install garage door** →
                                                  wood trim →
                    clean → [47] ⇢

32 Scheduling for Builders

On this particular job, all the interior trim is to be painted. Thus, no wood needs to be stained before being installed. The painting follows the trim installation.

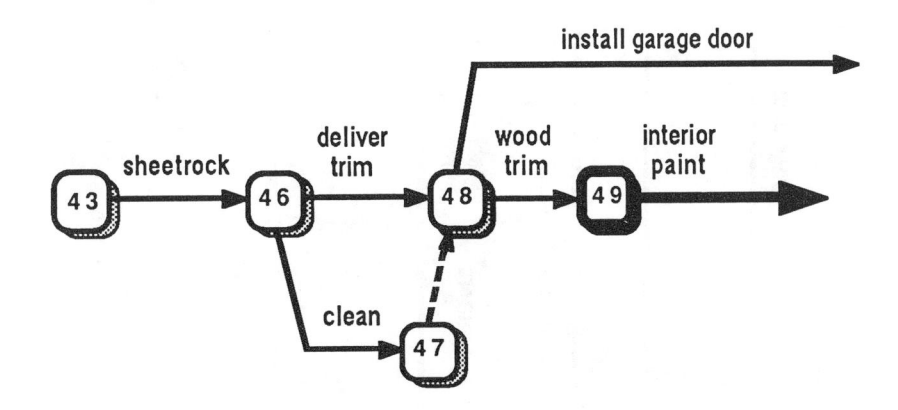

After the interior is painted, the interior work can begin in earnest. The wallpaper may be hung; the vinyl installed in the kitchen and baths; the fireplace masonry laid; and the cabinets, range hood, and mirrors delivered.

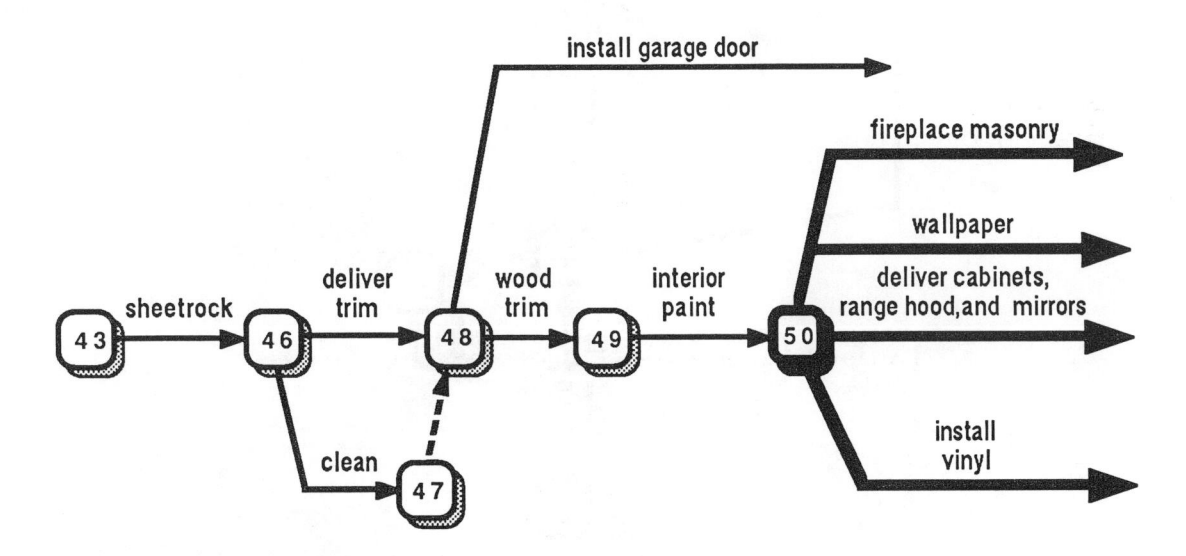

Next comes the installation of the cabinets, range hood, bathroom mirrors, and the base in the vinyl areas. As a matter of convenience, the HVAC trim will start and the dishwasher, kitchen stove, and light fixtures will be delivered at the same time (see Figure 8).

Chapter 2 The Planning Phase 33

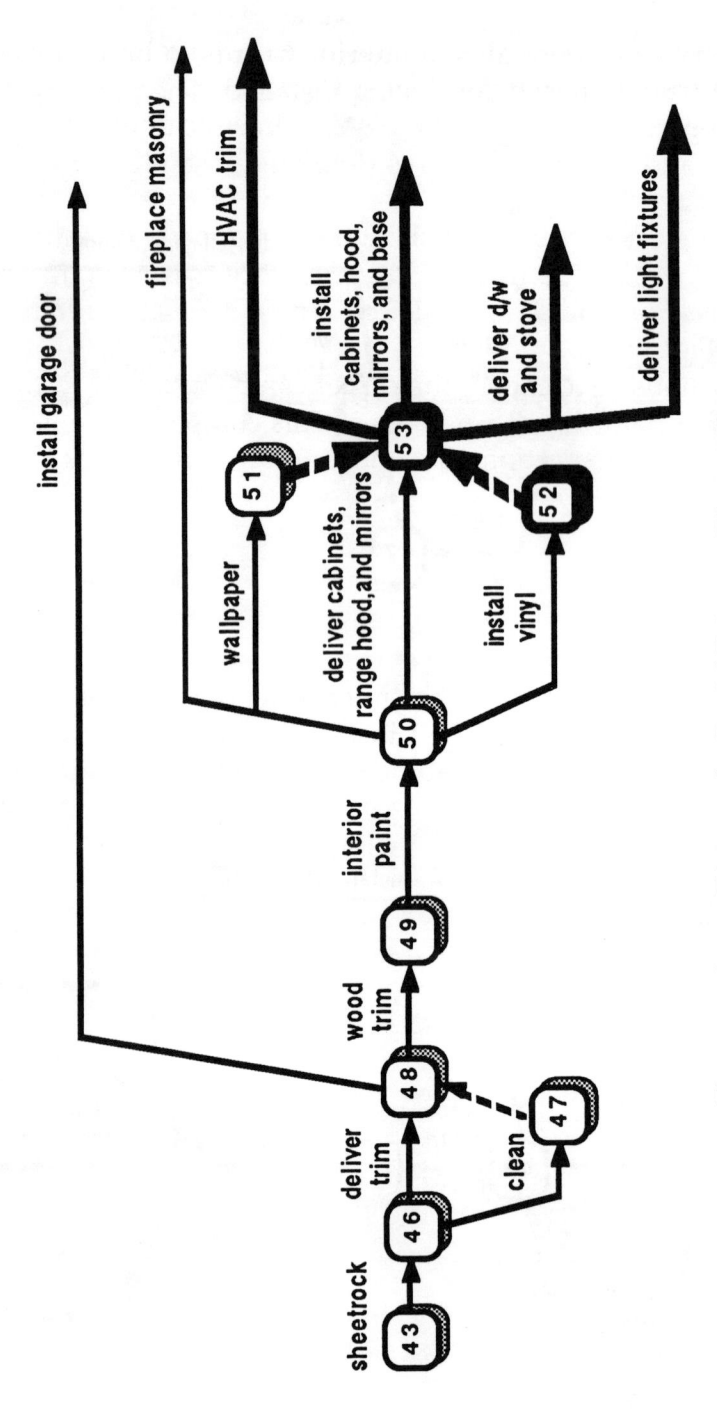

Figure 8   Arrow Diagram for Partial Trim-out Phase, House No. 2

34   Scheduling for Builders

The dishwasher needs to be on the job and the cabinets installed before the plumbing trim is started (see Figure 9).

Once the plumbing trim is complete, which includes setting the electric water heater, and the light fixtures delivered, the electrical trim-out can begin (see Figure 10).

When the electric trim is finished, the last general cleanup can be done but not before the HVAC trim and the fireplace masonry are finished. The electrical inspection and attic insulation can be done at the same time as the cleanup (see Figure 11).

After the house is cleaned, the carpet can be installed. After the carpet is laid, the final paint touch-up is done. This completes the list of activities except for the final inspection. The entire arrow diagram for House No. 2 is shown in Figures 12a-c.

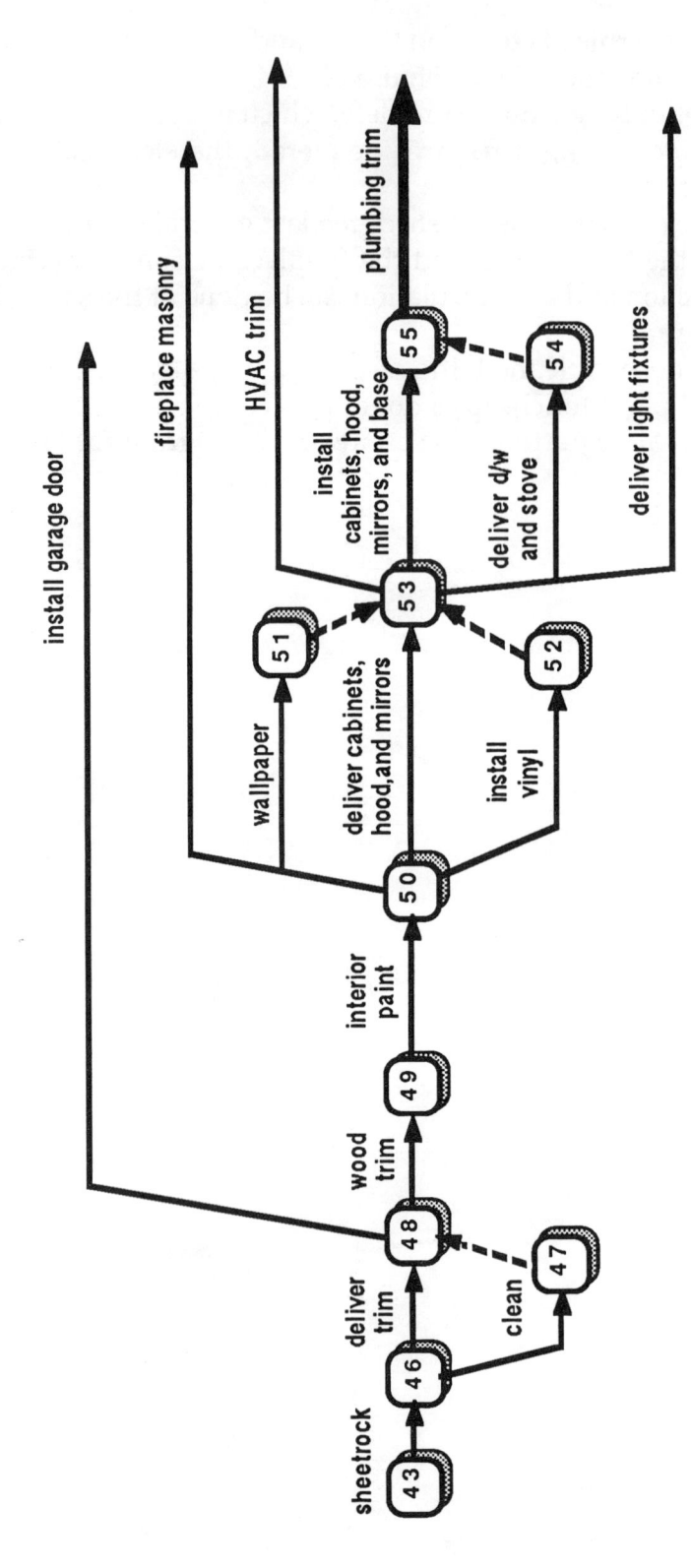

Figure 9 Arrow Diagram for Partial Trim-out Phase, House No. 2

36   Scheduling for Builders

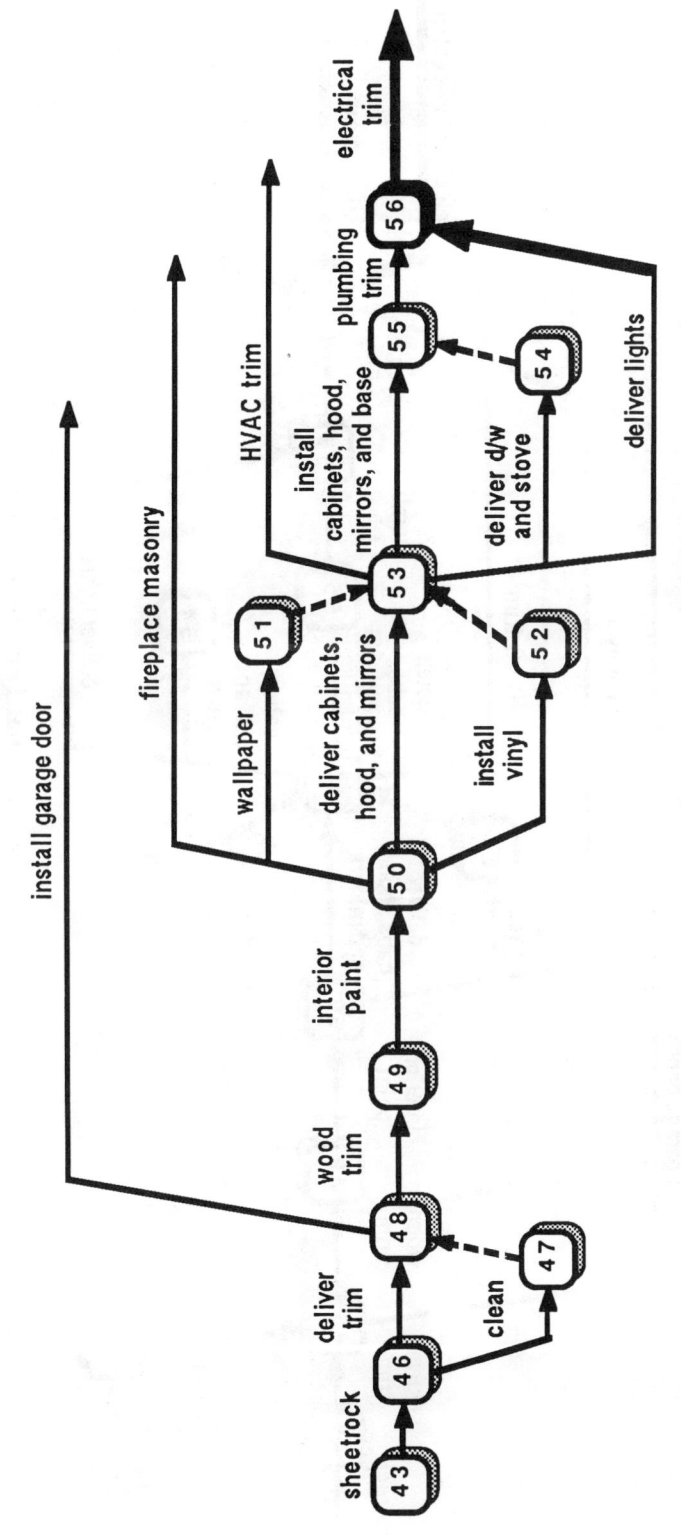

Figure 10 Arrow Diagram for Partial Trim-out Phase, House No. 2

Chapter 2 The Planning Phase   37

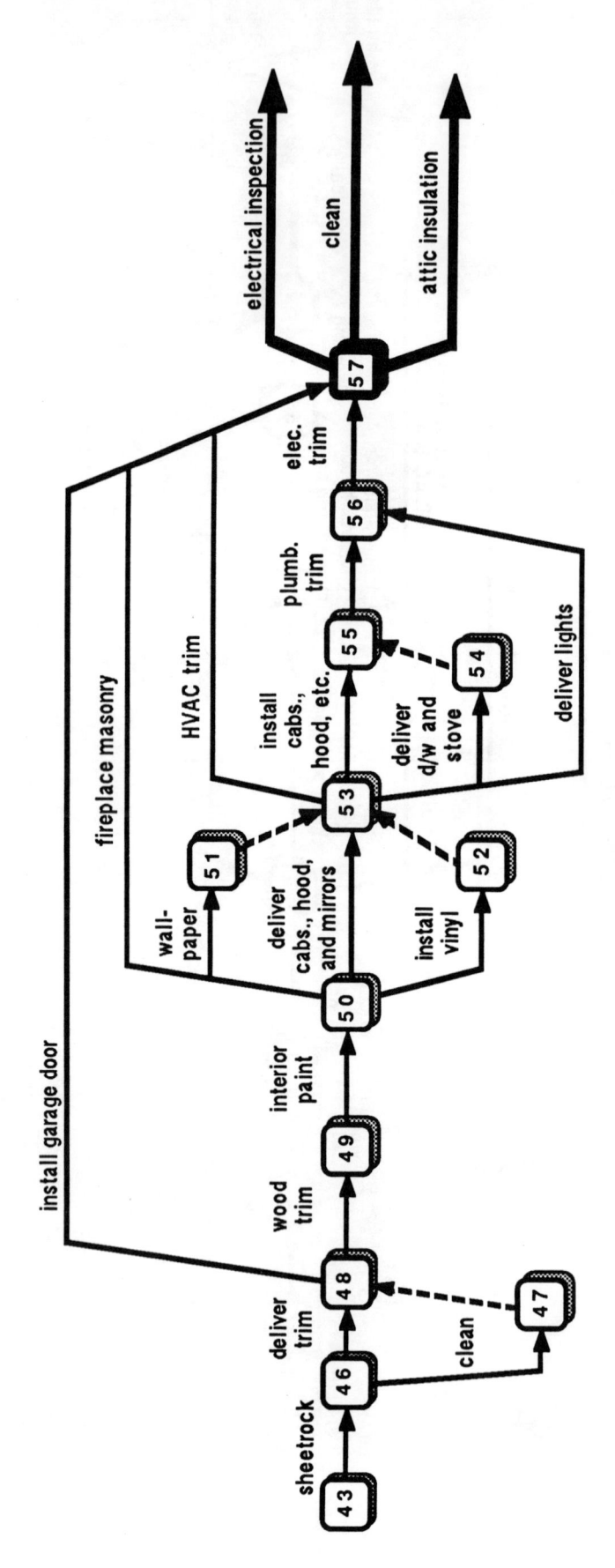

Figure 11 Arrow Diagram for Partial Trim-out Phase, House No. 2

38 Scheduling for Builders

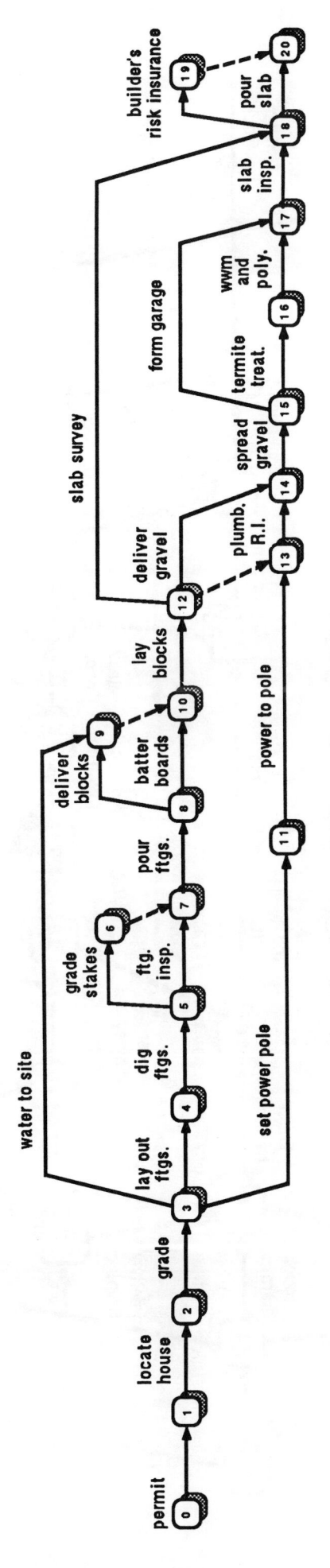

Figure 12a Complete Arrow Diagram, House No. 2

39

40 Scheduling for Builders

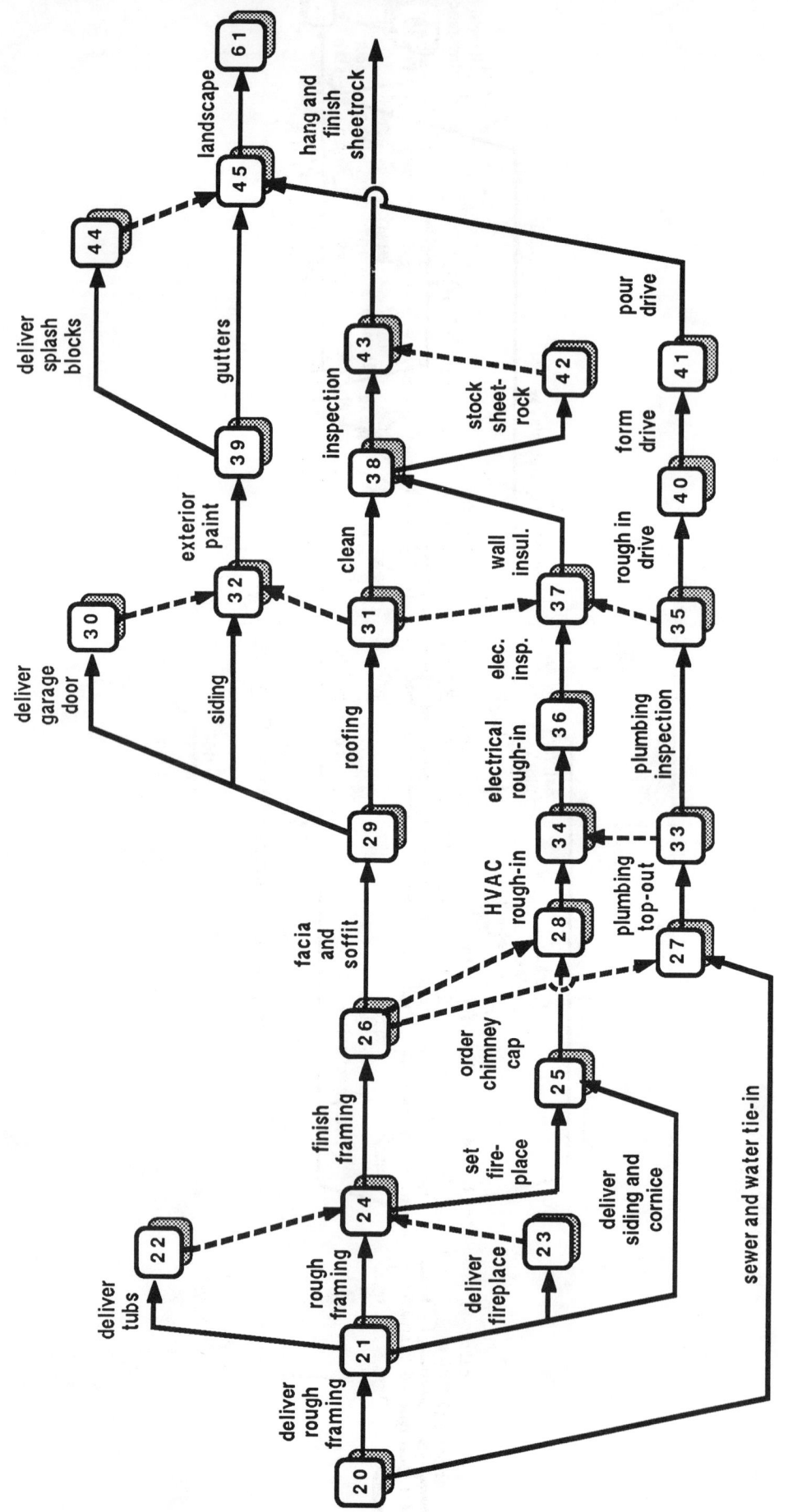

Figure 12b Complete Arrow Diagram, House No. 2

Figure 12c   Complete Arrow Diagram, House No. 2

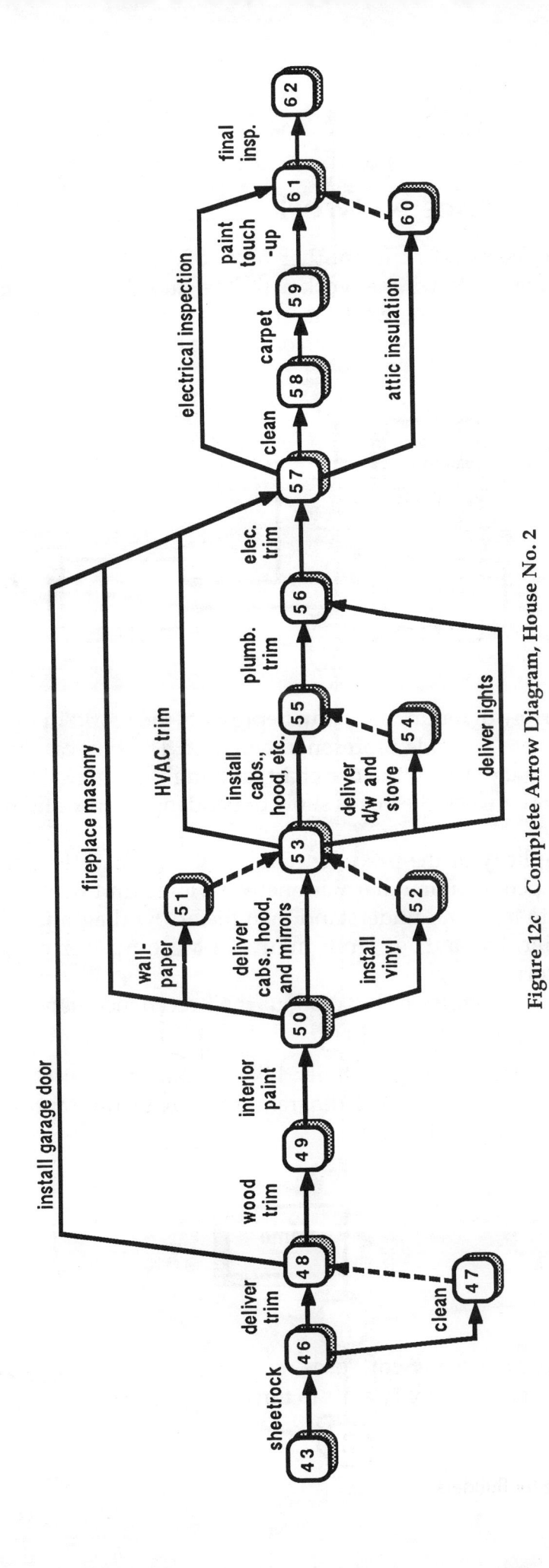

The Precedence Network

The precedence network is another form of CPM diagraming. Like the arrow diagram, it shows the work activities and their relationship to one another. A precedence network describes the activity in a box and shows the sequence of activities with interconnecting lines.

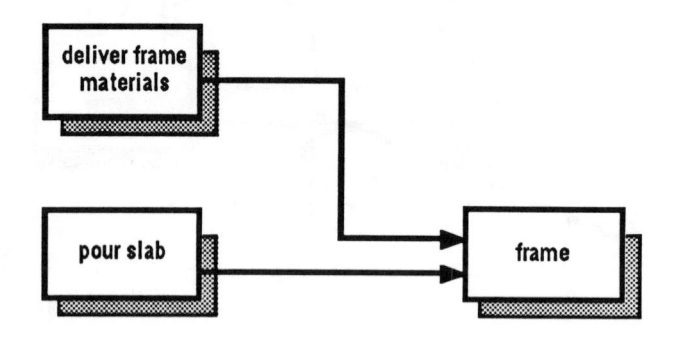

In the arrow diagram, the arrow represents the work. In the precedence network, the box or node represents the work. The box can be drawn to a time scale like the bar on the bar chart, although it's unnecessary. In either case, the lines between the boxes show dependencies only and do not represent any time.

The simplicity of the precedence network is one of its greatest advantages. Many people unfamiliar with network logic find the precedence network easier to read and understand than the arrow diagram. Also, as mentioned earlier, the output from many CPM computer programs is in precedence format.

The basic principles to learn about the precedence network are as follows:

1. A box represents an activity. Like the bar on a bar chart or the arrow in an arrow diagram, the box below represents the activity of framing.

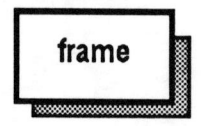

2. A precedence network uses no circles or event numbers to represent events or points in time.

3. Interconnecting lines between the boxes show the relationship between activities.

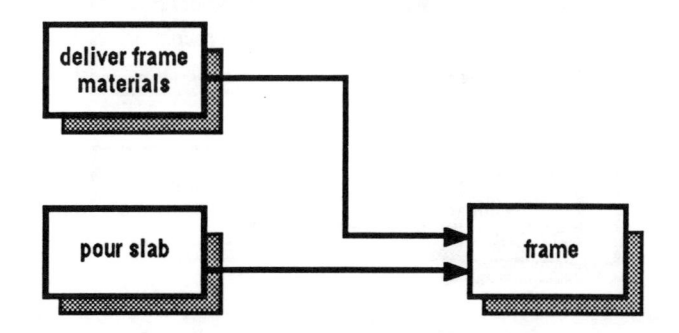

diagram: "deliver frame materials" and "pour slab" both lead to "frame"

In this example, when the frame materials are delivered, the next activity is framing. However, until the slab is poured, the framing cannot be done. In other words, all the activities with lines leading to a box must be complete before the work shown in that box can start.

As in the arrow diagram, each activity in a precedence network is subject to these questions:

- What activities must precede this activity?
- What activities can only follow this activity?
- What activities can be conducted simultaneously with this activity?

Another similarity with arrow diagrams is the use of both hard and soft constraints.

4. In a precedence network, the following representation is acceptable.

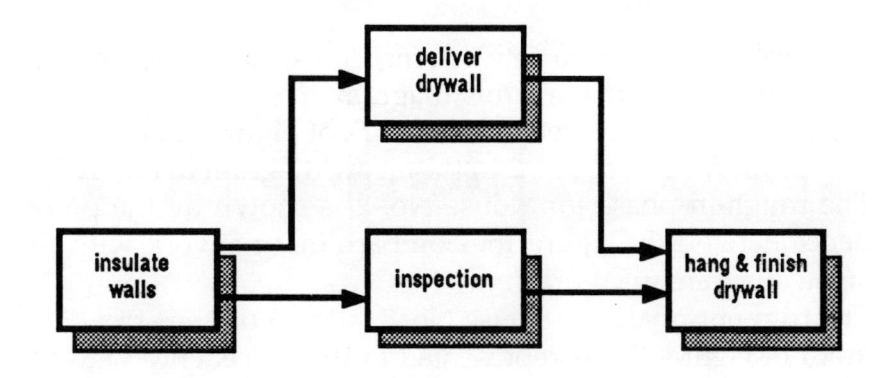

diagram: "insulate walls" leads to "deliver drywall" and "inspection"; both "deliver drywall" and "inspection" lead to "hang & finish drywall"

Chapter 2 The Planning Phase 43

Likewise, consider the four following activities:

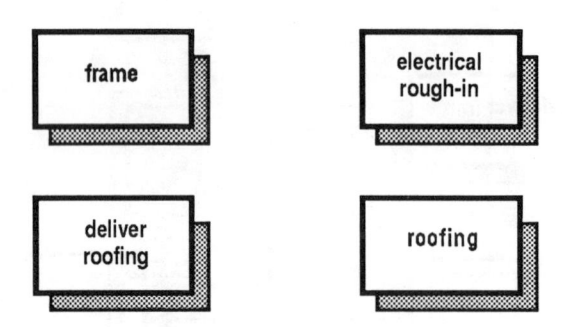

[frame] [electrical rough-in]

[deliver roofing] [roofing]

Then, consider how to show the following relationships:

- The framing must precede the electrical rough-in.
- The framing must be done before the roofing.
- The roofing must be delivered before it can be put on.

This sequence is shown as follows:

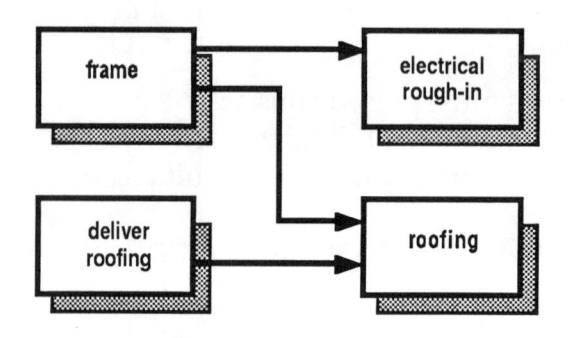

[frame] → [electrical rough-in]
[frame] → [roofing]
[deliver roofing] → [roofing]

Figures 13 through 16 appear on the following pages. Use them to make these comparisons:

- A complete precedence network for House No. 1 (Figures 13a-b) corresponds with the arrow diagram of Figure 2.
- Now compare the precedence network of Figures 14a-b for the slab phase for House No. 2 to the arrow diagram in Figure 3.
- The rough-in phase for House No. 2 is shown by the precedence network in Figure 15. Compare that network with the arrow diagram in Figure 7.
- The trim-out phase for House No. 2 (shown on the arrow diagram in Figure 12c) is represented in the precedence network of Figure 16.

44 Scheduling for Builders

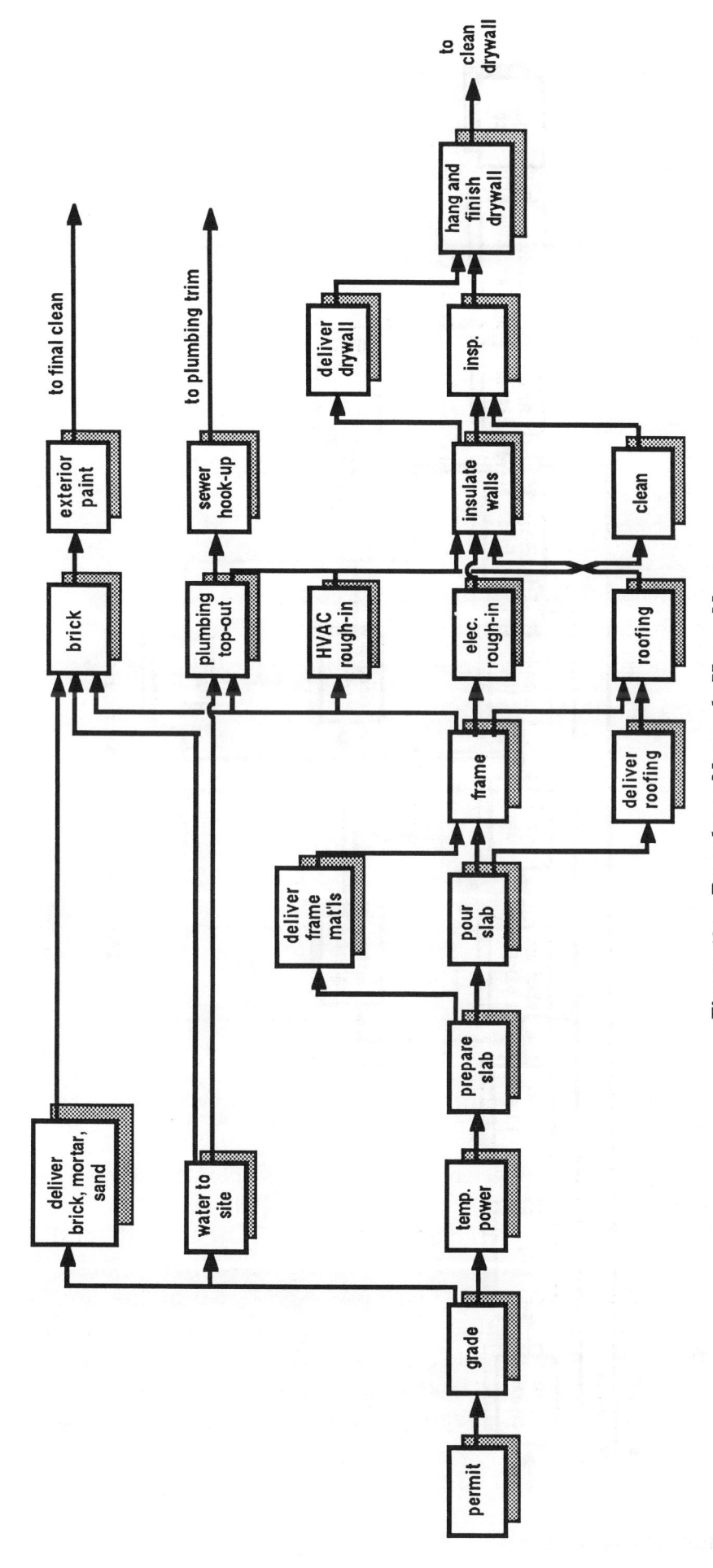

Figure 13a Precedence Network, House No. 1

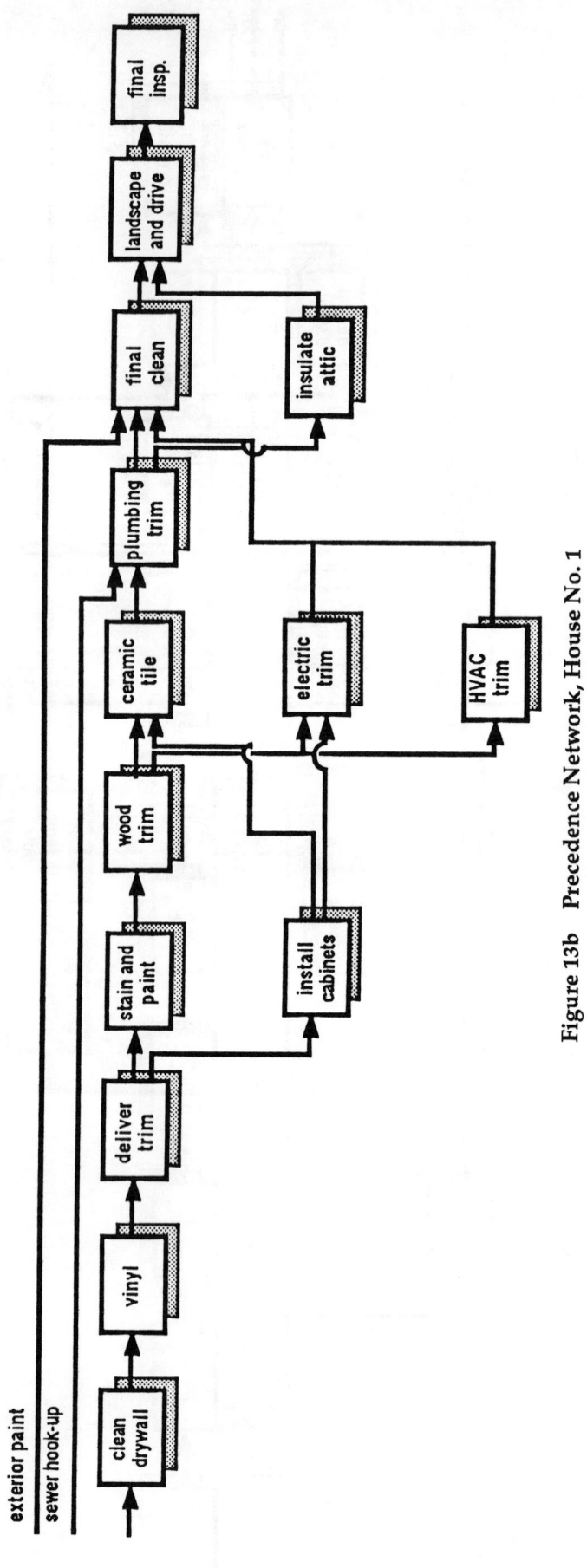

Figure 13b Precedence Network, House No. 1

46 Scheduling for Builders

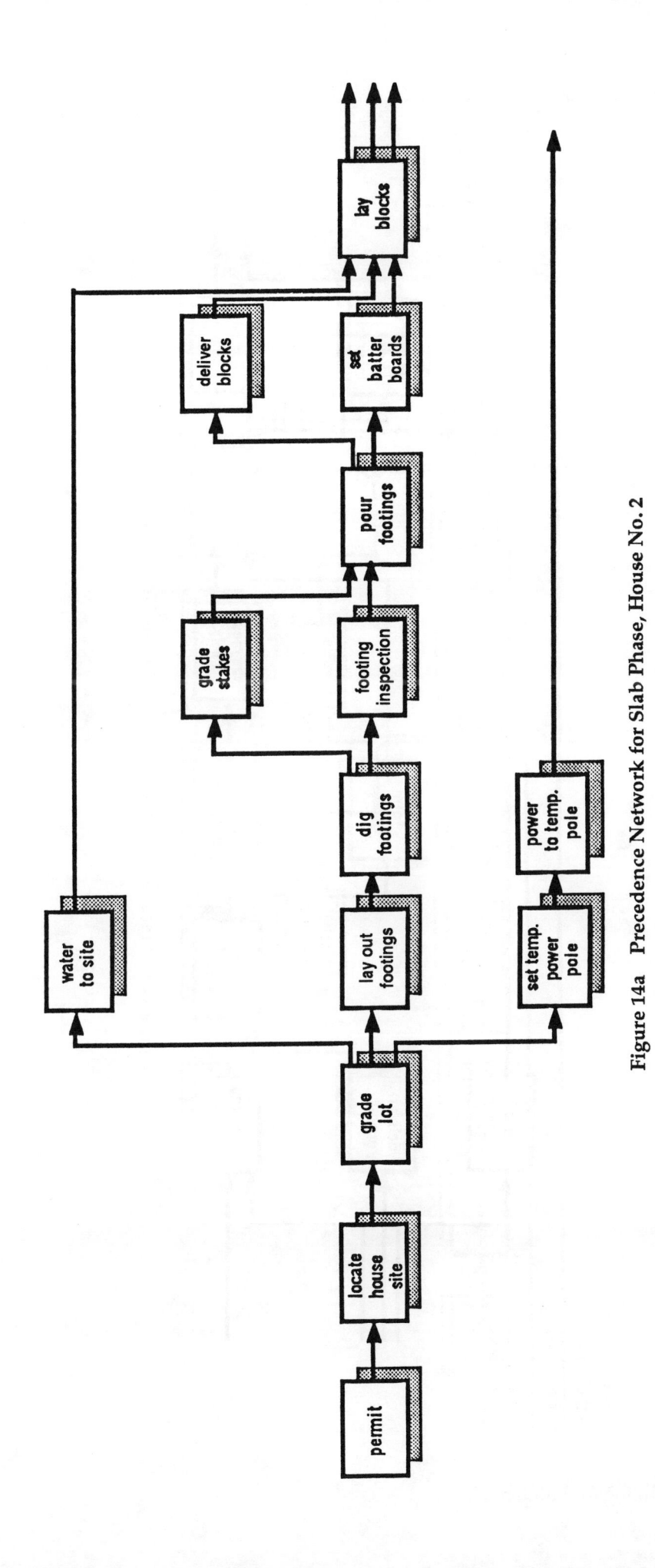

Figure 14a Precedence Network for Slab Phase, House No. 2

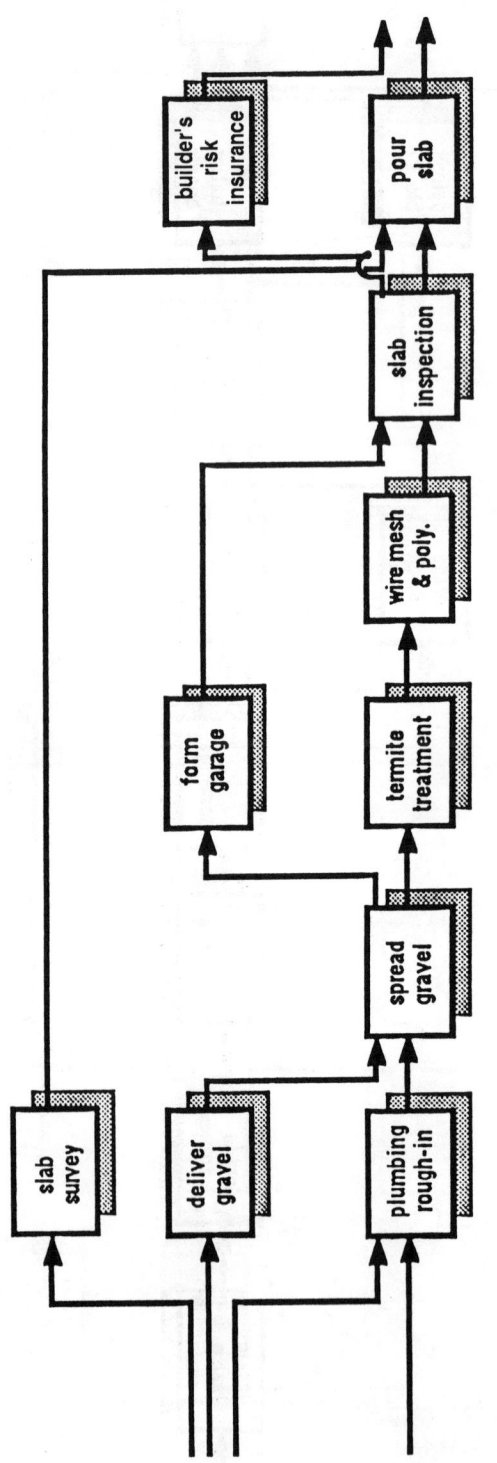

Figure 14b   Precedence Network for Slab Phase, House No. 2

48   Scheduling for Builders

Figure 15 Precedence Network for Rough-in Phase, House No. 2

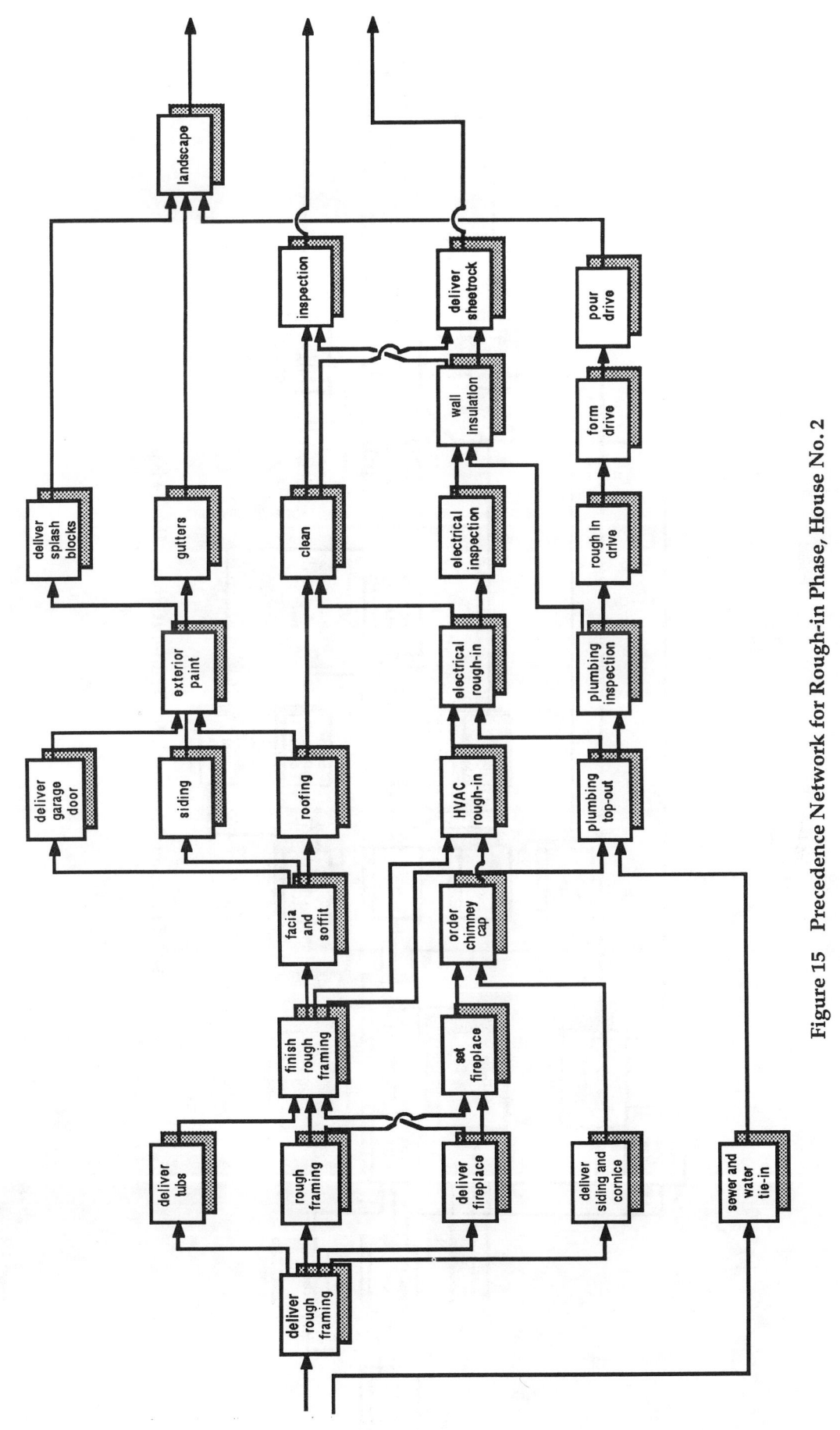

Chapter 2 The Planning Phase 49

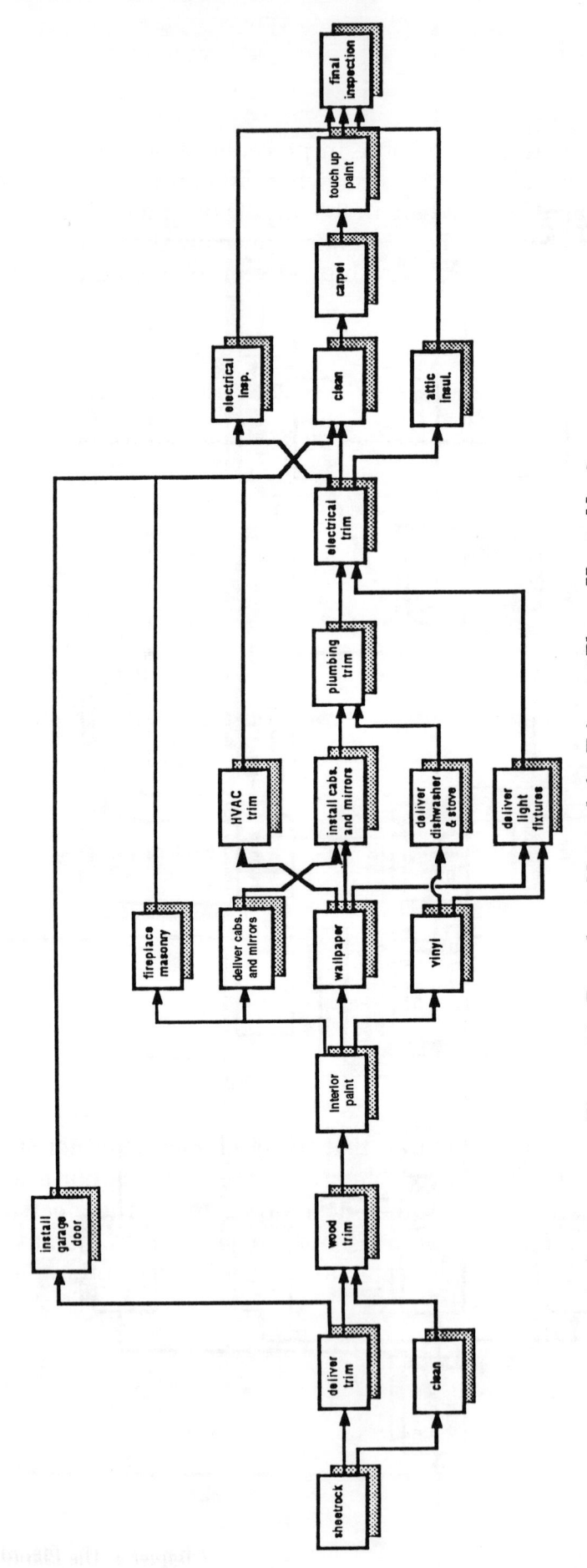

Figure 16 Precedence Network for Trim-out Phase, House No. 2

Another feature is available in precedence networks which, though powerful, makes the diagram somewhat difficult to read. An activity may be shown as starting anywhere in the middle of a preceding activity instead of only at its conclusion. For example, the arrow diagram for House No. 2 in Figure 12c shows the relationship between plumbing trim and electrical trim as follows:

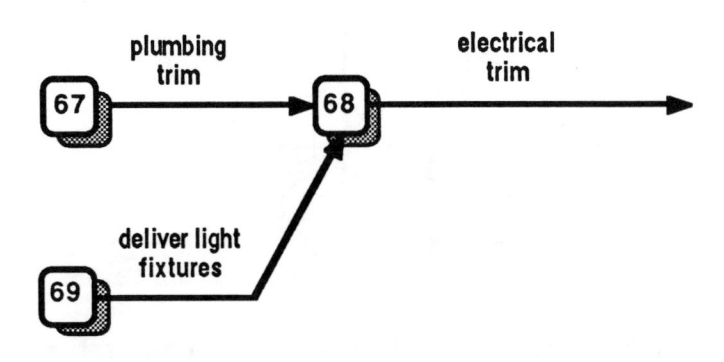

The precedence network for the same house in Figure 16 shows the same constraint.

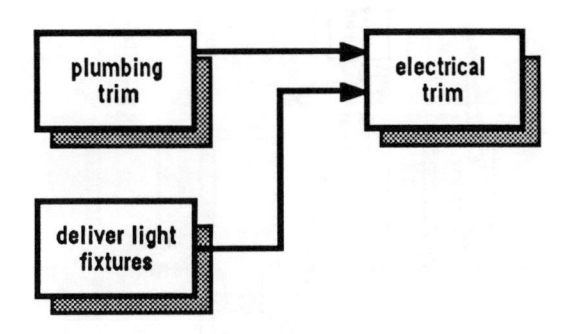

This representation means that the electrician may not start the trim-out until the plumber is completely finished. This is not exactly correct, however, because the plumber needs only to set the electric hot water heater before the electrician can hook power to it. In fact, as soon as the plumber sets the hot water heater, the electrician has nothing to wait for. In the following diagram, the arrow hooking the plumbing trim to the electrical trim comes from the middle or side of the box instead of the end. This indicates that the electrician can start after the plumber starts but before he or she finishes.

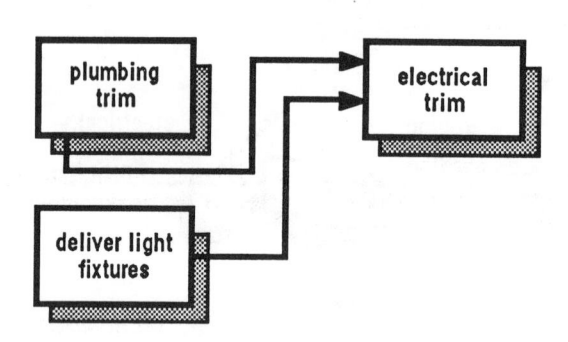

Also note what must happen before the carpenter sets the prefabricated fireplace in the following diagram:

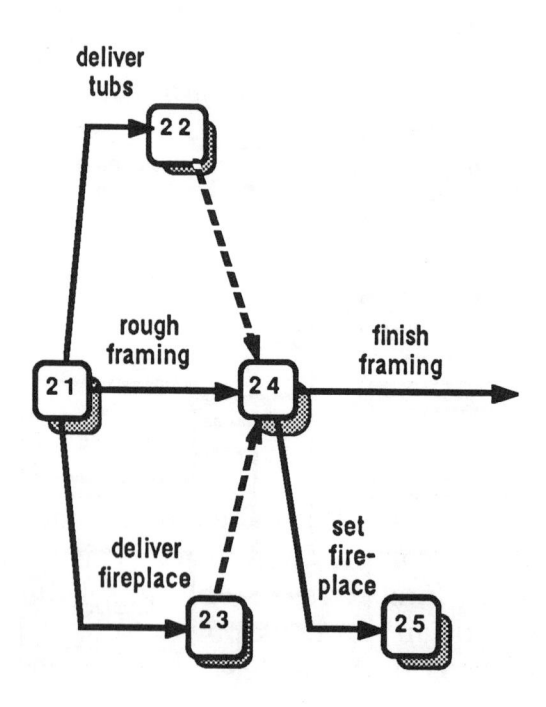

- The rough framing of the walls and roof must be done.
- The fireplace itself must be on site.
- The tubs must be on site.

52   Scheduling for Builders

There is no obvious reason for the tubs to be on site before the fireplace is set, yet that is what the diagram shows. To represent this properly on an arrow diagram, a circle and a dummy arrow should be added:

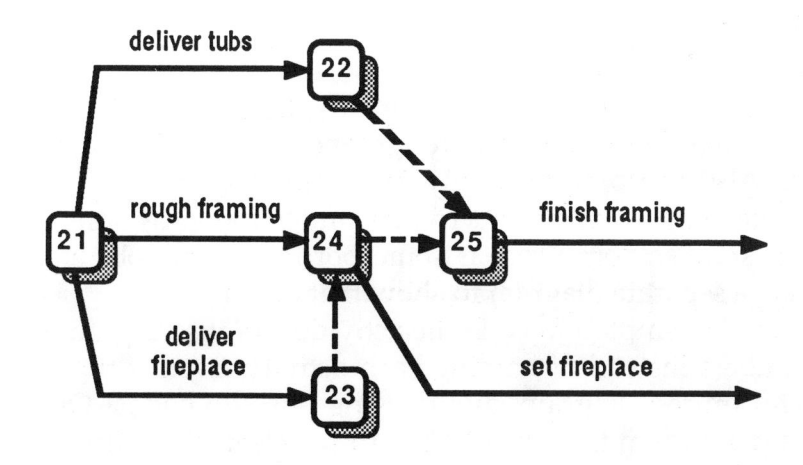

This new dummy arrow (24-25) takes no time. It simply shows that as soon as all the activities coming into event 24 are complete, you can move immediately down the dummy arrow to event 25. However, the following precedence network shows the same relationships:

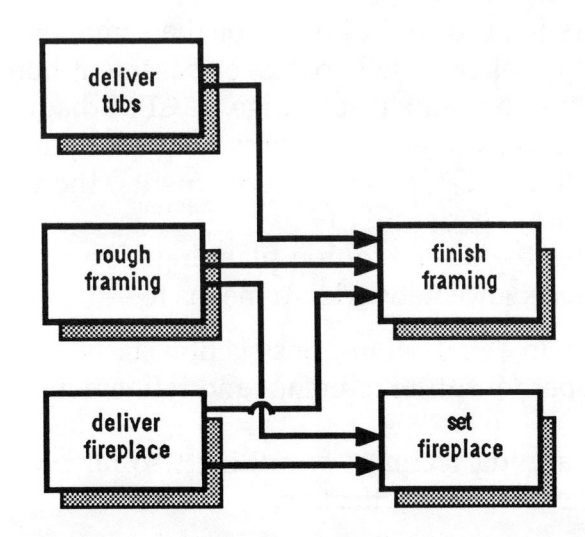

With either method, the more accurate the diagram is, the more complex it becomes. Some people like the activity on the arrow (i-j) method; others prefer the precedence method. You may wish to start with one

Chapter 2 The Planning Phase   53

method and then later try the other method as your skills improve and needs change.

Helpful Tips

Don't expect a CPM diagram drawn for the first time to be clear and concise. Usually the first drawing is rough and a redrawing takes care of the sloppiness. Also try not to draw any backward arrows.

Try to keep the number of activities under 100. Diagrams of more than 100 activities are seldom used. If some portion of the job requires greater detail, draw a separate diagram to show that detail.

You may be tempted to code the activities on the diagram by using letters or numbers instead of naming each activity. Even if the code appears on a legend on the diagram, avoid using obscure codes. One reason for drawing a diagram in the first place is to see clearly and improve the logic of the plan. For that to happen, the flow of the diagram must show all the activities properly named on the diagram.

The significant activities should go in the diagram's center so they become the backbone, while other, less significant activities revolve around them. This usually cuts the number of crossover arrows. Although it's not always possible to eliminate all the crossover arrows, keeping them to a minimum creates less confusion.

Most builders tend to build houses of the same general classification: houses on slabs, houses on crawl spaces, or basement houses. Builders also tend to build within the same price range. A CPM diagram of the way the house should have been built can be very helpful. By using hindsight and drawing a new diagram with smart refinements, the builder can benefit more fully from past experience.

This concludes the discussion on planning. The drawing of the arrow diagram or the precedence network is a means to—

- look at a job in detail before construction starts
- plan on paper for future reference and refinements

Using the planning techniques outlined so far will almost certainly make managerial efforts more effective.

CHAPTER 3

The Scheduling Phase

The scheduling phase of a project can only be done when the planning phase is finished and the arrow diagram or precedence network shows what the builder is going to do. Short, simple diagrams, however, may be drawn to a time scale as the planning logic progresses on simple jobs. But with more complex jobs, it is better to plan first and schedule later.

The builder must decide what unit of time to use when scheduling the project. Whether the unit is hours, half days, days, or weeks, the same unit of time must be used throughout the network. On most large commercial projects, the unit is usually days. On residential projects, the use of half days is common. For scheduling shorter, internal segments, the time unit may more conveniently be reduced to hours.

In residential construction, many activities take only an hour or so. For example, for most houses it takes less than a whole day to stake out the house location, set the grade stakes in the footing trench, or treat the soil for termite protection. If the builder uses a minimum time unit of one day, the resulting schedule will be unrealistically long unless short duration activities are omitted or combined with other activities.

As discussed earlier, relationships with subcontractors and material suppliers usually improve when a builder uses formal scheduling methods. However, for the builder to benefit in this way, the schedule must be realistic.

Activity Duration

The first step in working out a schedule is to assign time limits to each activity based on experience and knowledge of local conditions.

The builder should get an estimate from each subcontractor of how long the work will take. Sometimes, busy subcontractors will move on to a job and do a little work, thereby staking claim, and then pull off to finish or start another job. Getting a time estimate at the start helps to curtail this behavior.

A good rule to follow is that no activity should be scheduled for less than half a day. Any task that takes less time should be rounded up to a half day. For example, to ride to the job and set the grade stakes may only take an hour, but a half day is used. Likewise, if any activity is expected to take five or six hours, such as grading the lot, a whole day is allowed.

The times estimated for the activities for the slab phase of House No. 2 are as follows:

Activity	Time in Days
1. Obtain permit.	½
2. Establish house location.	½
3. Grade lot.	1
4. Lay out footings.	½
5. Dig footings.	½
6. Set grade stakes in footing trench.	½
7. Get footing inspection.	½
8. Pour footings.	½
9. Set batter boards.	½
10. Deliver header blocks, mortar mix, and sand.	½
11. Lay blocks.	½
12. Rough in underslab plumbing.	1
13. Deliver gravel.	½
14. Spread gravel.	½
15. Treat for termites.	½
16. Form garage.	½
17. Place welded wire mesh and polyethylene.	½
18. Get slab inspection.	½
19. Survey slab.	1
20. Pour slab.	1
21. Get water to site.	1
22. Set temporary power pole.	½
23. Bring power to temporary pole.	2
24. Get builder's risk insurance.	½

These durations may or may not come close to those with which most builders are accustomed. They are presented only to illustrate a method and are not given as a guide on how to schedule every home.

Time Computations

Once the duration of each activity has been determined, meaningful time computations can be made. These computations may be done in several ways.

To begin the time computations, the morning of the first day is designated as time zero since no work has been done. So, referring back to Figure 3, the earliest the activity 0-1, permit, can begin is time zero and the earliest it can finish, assuming that it takes half a day to do, is time ½. In other words, the early start for activity 0-1 is zero and the early finish is ½. Likewise, the early start for activity 1-2, locate house, is ½ and the early finish is 1. If it takes half a day to get the building permit and the house location cannot be staked out until the permit is obtained, the earliest locating the house can begin is at time ½ or midway through the first day. Also, if the stakeout takes half a day, the earliest that this activity can finish is at time 1 or the end of the first day.

Referring again to Figure 3, activity 2-3, grade, cannot start until the beginning of the second day. Both the end of the first day and the beginning of the second day are called time 1 because only one complete work day has passed. From the project's standpoint, since no work has been done, both points represent the same point in time. Therefore, the early start for activity 2-3 is 1. The early finish is determined by adding the duration of the activity to the early start. This results in an early finish of 2.

From event 3, the work branches out with the start of three separate activities: 3-9, water to the site; 3-4, lay out footings; and 3-11, set temporary power pole. Since all three of these activities can start when the grading is finished, their early start time is the same as the early finish time for grading at time 2 or after two complete days of work. The early finish for each of these activities is found by adding their respective durations to the early start time. This computation results in an early finish time of 3 for getting water to the site and 2½ for both laying out footings and setting the temporary power pole.

Since activity 4-5, dig footings, depends only on the finish of activity 3-4, lay out footings, it may begin at time 2½, which is the early finish for activity 3-4. The early finish for activity 4-5 is then found to be its early start, 2½, plus its duration, ½, which equals 3. The early start time for both activities 5-6, grade stakes, and 5-7, footing inspection, is 3. Since their duration time is ½, they each have an early finish time of 3½.

Following the same procedure, activity 7-8, pour footings, has an early start time of 3½ and an early finish time of 4. Likewise, activities 8-9, deliver blocks, and 8-10, batter boards, have early start times of 4 and early finish times of 4½. For activity 10-12, lay blocks, to start, all the arrows coming into event 10 must be complete. In other words, the batter boards must be up, the blocks must be delivered, and the water must be to the site. Deliver blocks and batter boards both finish at 4½ days while water to the site finishes at 3 days.

In determining the early start for an activity that is constrained by more than one prior activity, use the latest finish date of the prior activities. In this case, activity 10-12, lay blocks, cannot start until 4½ days at which time all the constraining activities are done.

The complete early start and finish times for the slab construction of House No. 2 are as follows:

Activity	i	j	Duration	Early Start	Early Finish
permit	0	1	½	0	½
locate house site	1	2	½	½	1
grade	2	3	1	1	2
lay out footings	3	4	½	2	2½
water to site	3	9	1	2	3
dig footings	4	5	½	2½	3
grade stakes	5	6	½	3	3½
footing inspection	5	7	½	3	3½
pour footings	7	8	½	3½	4
deliver blocks	8	9	½	4	4½
batter boards	8	10	½	4	4½
lay blocks	10	12	½	4½	5
set power pole	3	11	½	2	2½
power to pole	11	13	2	2½	4½
slab survey	12	18	1	5	6
deliver gravel	12	14	½	5	5½
plumbing rough-in	13	14	1	5	6
spread gravel	14	15	½	6	6½
termite treatment	15	16	½	6½	7
form garage	15	17	½	6½	7
WWM & poly.	16	17	½	7	7½
slab inspection	17	18	½	7½	8
pour slab	18	20	1	8	9
bldr's risk insur.	18	19	½	8	8½

Thus, by making a forward pass through Figure 3, early start and finish times may be established. Once these parameters are determined, a CPM diagram can be drawn to a time scale. First, draw event zero at time zero. Next, draw the activities to the appropriate scale according to their durations and follow the same logical progression just outlined.

By using this technique, the arrow diagram in Figure 3 can be produced with a time scale for the slab construction of House No. 2 as shown in Figure 17. According to the diagram in Figure 17, nine days are required to complete the work because some activities occur at the same time as others. Note that some arrows are part solid and part dashed.

Just as each activity has an early start and finish time, each activity has a late start and finish time. The late start time is the latest possible time that an activity can start and not delay the finish of the project. Likewise, the late finish time is the latest possible time that an activity can finish and not delay the finish of the project. The late start and finish times of each activity can be determined by making a pass backward through Figure 17 similar to the forward pass described earlier.

Since the slab project shown in Figure 17 ends at day 9, the late finish of the two activities, pour slab (18-20) and builder's risk insurance (19-20), ending at event 20 is 9. Builder's risk insurance actually ends at event 19, but the arrow from 19 to 20 is a dummy put into the diagram to keep these two activities from having the same identification numbers. Therefore, since this dummy arrow takes no time, both activities end at event 20.

Working backward, the late start of activity 18-20, pour slab, is 9 minus the duration, 1, or 8. The late start for activity 18-19, builder's risk insurance, is 9 minus ½ or 8½. For the project's finish not to be delayed, both activities ending at event 18—activity 12-18, slab survey, and activity 17-18, slab inspection—must be finished at time 8 or the end of the eighth day. Since both these activities must be finished by time 8, this then is their late finish. Subtracting their durations, the late start for activity 17-18 is 8 minus ½ or 7½ and the late start for activity 12-18 is 8 minus 1 or 7.

A complete listing of early start, early finish, late start, and late finish for the slab phase of House No. 2 is as follows:

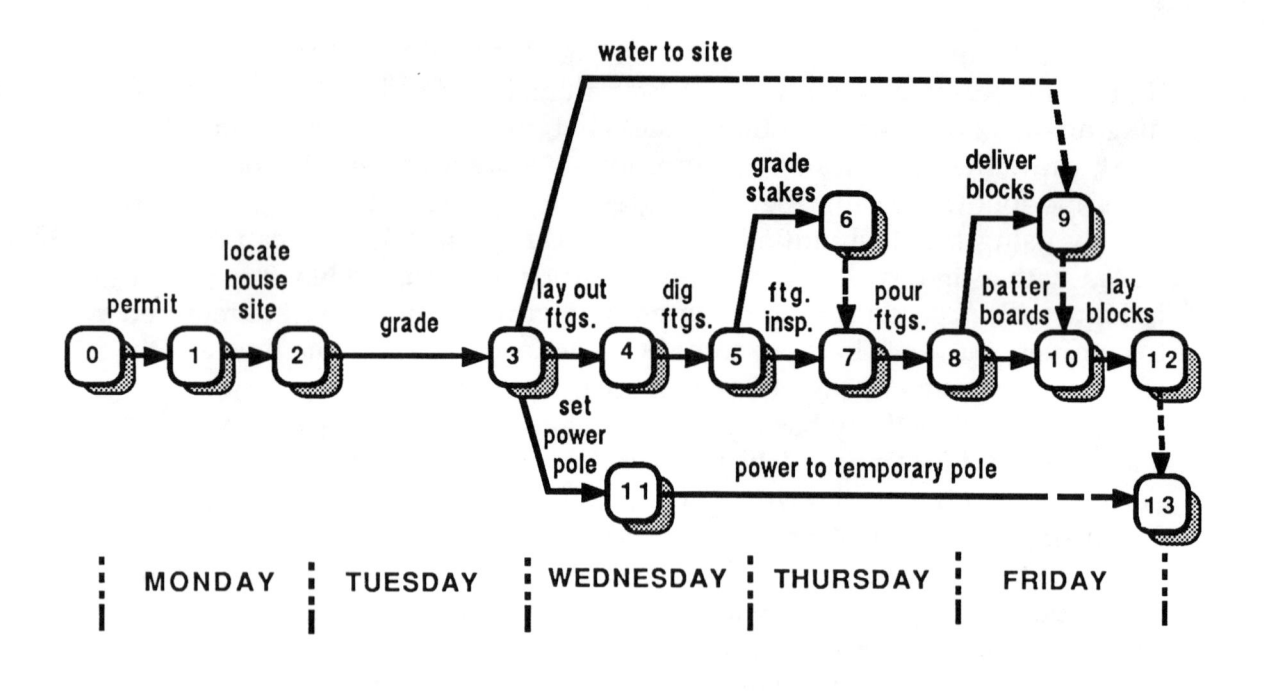

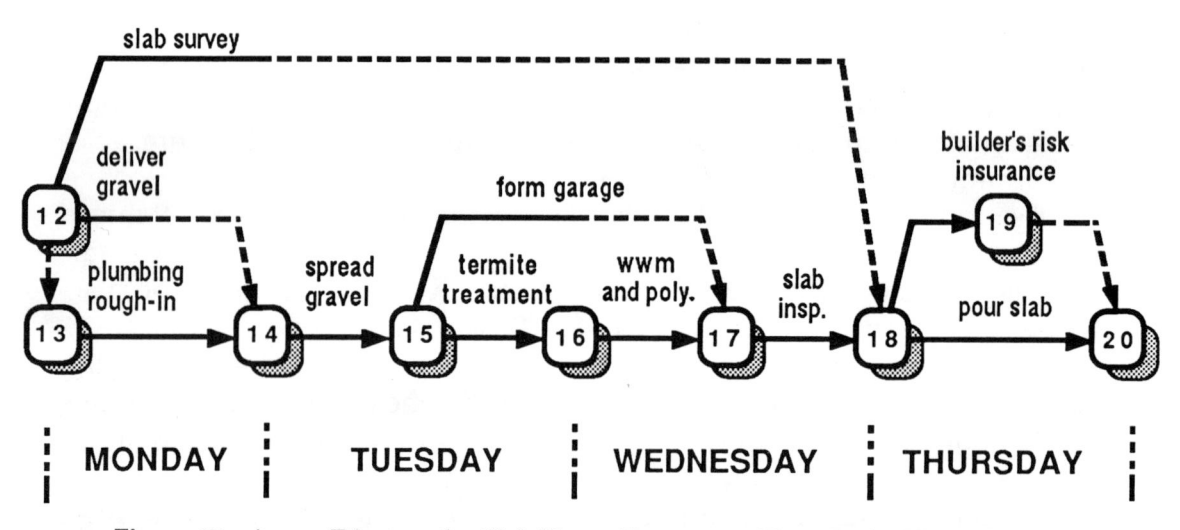

Figure 17 Arrow Diagram for Slab Phase, Drawn to a Time Scale, House No. 2

60 Scheduling for Builders

Activity	i	j	Duration	Early Start	Early Finish	Late Start	Late Finish
permit	0	1	½	0	½	0	½
locate house site	1	2	½	½	1	½	1
grade	2	3	1	1	2	1	2
lay out footings	3	4	½	2	2½	2	2½
water to site	3	9	1	2	3	3½	4½
dig footings	4	5	½	2½	3	2½	3
grade stakes	5	6	½	3	3½	3	3½
footing inspection	5	7	½	3	3½	3	3½
pour footings	7	8	½	3½	4	3½	4
deliver blocks	8	9	½	4	4½	4	4½
batter boards	8	10	½	4	4½	4	4½
lay blocks	10	12	½	4½	5	4½	5
set power pole	3	11	½	2	2½	2½	3
power to pole	11	13	2	2½	4½	3	5
slab survey	12	18	1	5	6	7	8
deliver gravel	12	14	½	5	5½	5½	6
plumbing rough-in	13	14	1	5	6	5	6
spread gravel	14	15	½	6	6½	6	6½
termite treatment	15	16	½	6½	7	6½	7
form garage	15	17	½	6½	7	7	7½
WWM & poly.	16	17	½	7	7½	7	7½
slab inspection	17	18	½	7½	8	7½	8
pour slab	18	20	1	8	9	8	9
bldr's risk insur.	18	19	½	8	8½	8½	9

Computer programs that are written for CPM diagraming basically do two things: (1) Given the first four columns in the preceding table, activity, i, j, and duration, they calculate the start and finish times. (2) They also plot the corresponding diagram.

Computers, though, cannot determine the logic necessary to draw an arrow diagram or precedence network. Computers can only calculate start and finish dates and draw the CPM diagram after someone has determined the sequence of activities. The builder must decide if such results from the computer justify the effort required.

The Critical Path

Out of the 24 activities listed, 17, if delayed, would delay the slab being ready. These 17 activities are as follows:

- Obtain permit.
- Locate house site.
- Grade.
- Lay out footings.
- Dig footings.
- Set grade stakes.
- Inspect footings.
- Pour footings.
- Deliver blocks.
- Set batter boards.
- Lay blocks.
- Rough in plumbing.
- Spread gravel.
- Treat for termites.
- Place welded wire mesh and polyethylene.
- Inspect slab.
- Pour slab.

These activities are critical to the timely completion of this portion of the job. The path of these activities is called the critical path. Critical path activities form a solid line from start to finish in the network. After drawing a CPM diagram, it is helpful to darken the lines of the critical path to show which activities are most important. In addition, to avoid delaying the job, the early and late start times for critical path activities must be the same. If an activity with a partially dashed line (other than a dummy activity) is on a particular path, then it is not a critical path. One benefit of determining the critical path is to identify which activities to expedite to ensure the timely completion of the project.

Float

Refer to the diagram in Figure 17 again. What will happen to the total completion time if the water to the site takes two days instead of one? The answer is that nothing will happen since this activity has a day and a half of extra time available. This extra time is called float. Activities with float have partially dashed lines or are on a path with such activities. The amount of float an activity has can be determined by subtracting the early start time from the late start time. Seven out of 24 activities in the network have float:

Activity	Float in Days
13. Deliver gravel.	½
16. Form garage.	½
19. Survey slab.	2
21. Get water to site.	1½
22. Set temporary power pole.	½
23. Bring power to pole.	½
24. Get builder's risk insurance.	½

The concept that some activities are critical and some have float is one of the more important reasons to use CPM diagraming. Activities that are critical and those that have float can be determined from the table showing early and late start and finish times. Again, remember that the early and late start times for critical activities are the same. In other words, these activities must start as soon as they can in order not to delay the job.

Notice the two activities in Figure 17 forming the path from event 3 to event 13—set power pole and bring power to pole. These activities have a half day float, but that doesn't mean that each one can be delayed by a half day. If setting the temporary power pole takes one whole day instead of a half day and bringing the power to the pole takes two and a half days instead of two, then the plumbing rough-in will start half a day late, delaying the project. So the float of a half day is for the whole loop 3-11 and 11-13 and not for each activity individually.

The critical path is that sequence of activities through the network that takes the longest time. It is usually thought of as a single path. However, critical activities can run simultaneously. For example, the network in Figure 17 has two such loops where concurrent critical activities branch and rejoin. Both the footing inspection and the grade stake placement are critical. Likewise, the block delivery and batter boards are critical. A delay in any of these activities would push the subsequent activities back.

Most construction projects have cost estimates for various phases of the job. Final costs seldom match estimated costs. Likewise, a CPM diagram drawn before a job starts is just an estimate and the as-built sequence of events and times is likely to be different. Therefore, the real critical path may not be the one that is first drawn. If some particular loop with float uses more than its extra time, that activity will become critical. As an example, in Figure 17, if water cannot get to the site before the masons are ready, the water-to-site activity will become critical. The path through lay out footings, dig footings, inspect footings and place grade stakes, pour footings, set batter boards, and deliver blocks will no longer be critical because these steps will have already been completed.

To finish House No. 2 that was started in Figure 17 requires the following list of activities. As before, different circumstances might change the times, such as the job size, the number of workers for each activity, or the time of year.

Rough-in Phase, House No. 2

Activity	Time in Days
25. Deliver rough framing.	½
26. Rough framing.	2
27. Deliver siding and cornice.	½
28. Deliver fireplace.	½
29. Deliver tubs.	½
30. Finish framing.	2
31. Set fireplace.	½
32. Tie in sewer and water.	1
33. Order chimney cap.	½
34. Install facia and soffit.	1
35. Install siding.	2
36. Install roofing.	2
37. Deliver garage door.	½
38. Top out plumbing.	1½
39. Rough in HVAC.	1
40. Inspect plumbing.	½
41. Paint exterior.	2
42. Rough in electrical work.	1
43. Inspect electrical work.	½
44. Install gutters.	½
45. Insulate walls.	½
46. Clean up.	1
47. Rough in drive.	½
48. Form drive.	½
49. Pour drive.	½
50. Deliver splash blocks.	½
51. Inspect.	½
52. Stock sheetrock.	½
53. Landscape.	2

Trim-out Phase, House No. 2

Activity	Time in Days
54. Hang and finish sheetrock.	4
55. Clean up sheetrock.	½
56. Deliver wood trim.	½
57. Install wood trim.	1½
58. Install garage door.	½
59. Paint interior.	3
60. Hang wallpaper.	1
61. Install vinyl.	½
62. Deliver cabinets, mirrors, and range hood.	½
63. Install cabinets, mirrors, and range hood.	1
64. Deliver dishwasher and stove.	½
65. Install fireplace masonry.	1
66. Trim out HVAC.	1
67. Trim out plumbing.	2
68. Trim out electrical work.	1½
69. Deliver lights.	½
70. Inspect electrical work.	½
71. Clean up.	1
72. Touch up paint.	½
73. Insulate attic.	½
74. Carpet.	1
75. Conduct final inspection.	½

A CPM diagram for the rough-in phase for House No. 2 is shown in Figure 18 and the trim-out phase for House No. 2 is shown in Figure 19. Both figures are drawn to a time scale.

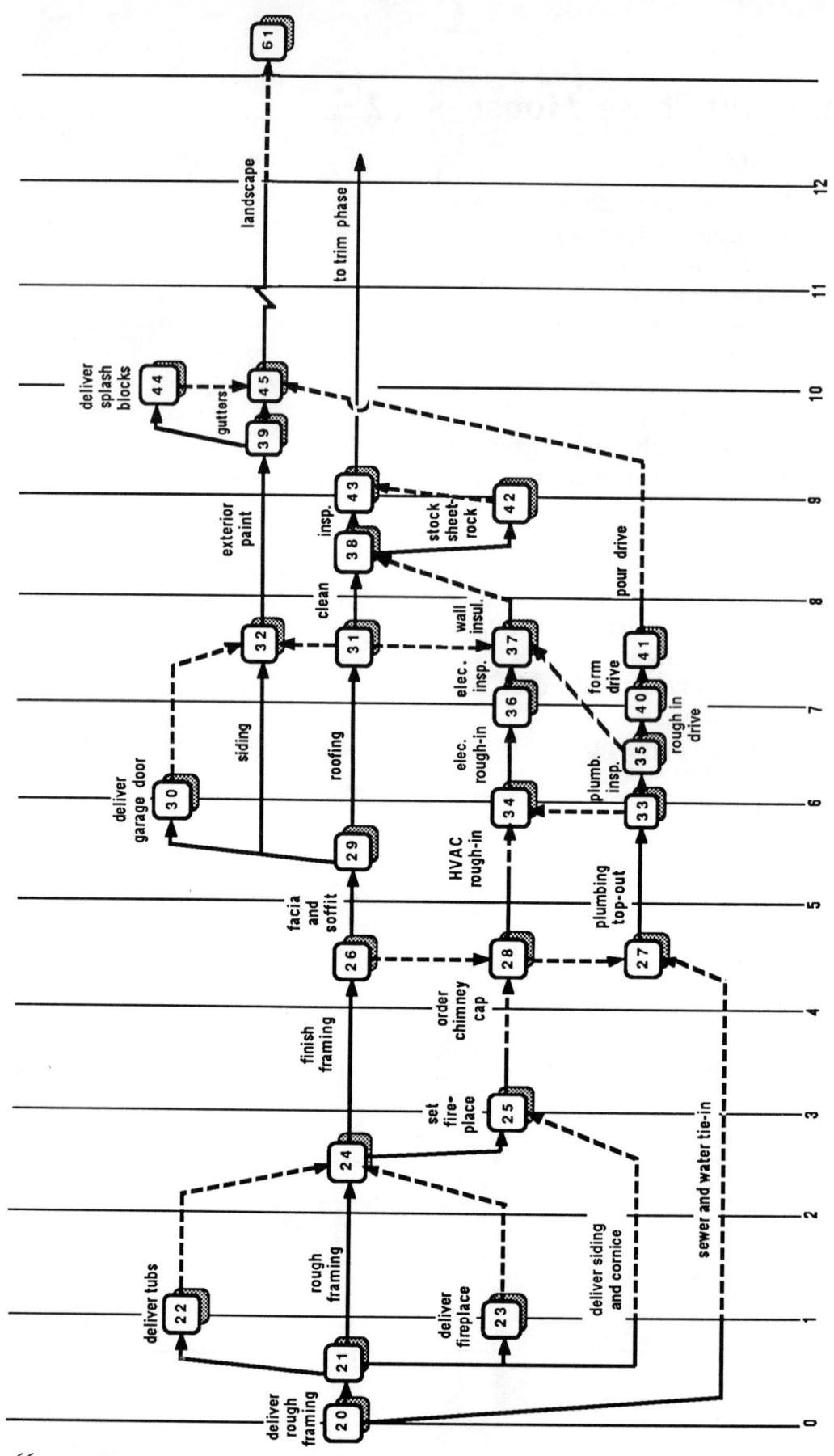

Figure 18 Arrow Diagram for Rough-in Phase, Drawn to a Time Scale, House No. 2

Figure 19 Arrow Diagram for Trim-out Phase, Drawn to a Time Scale, House No. 2

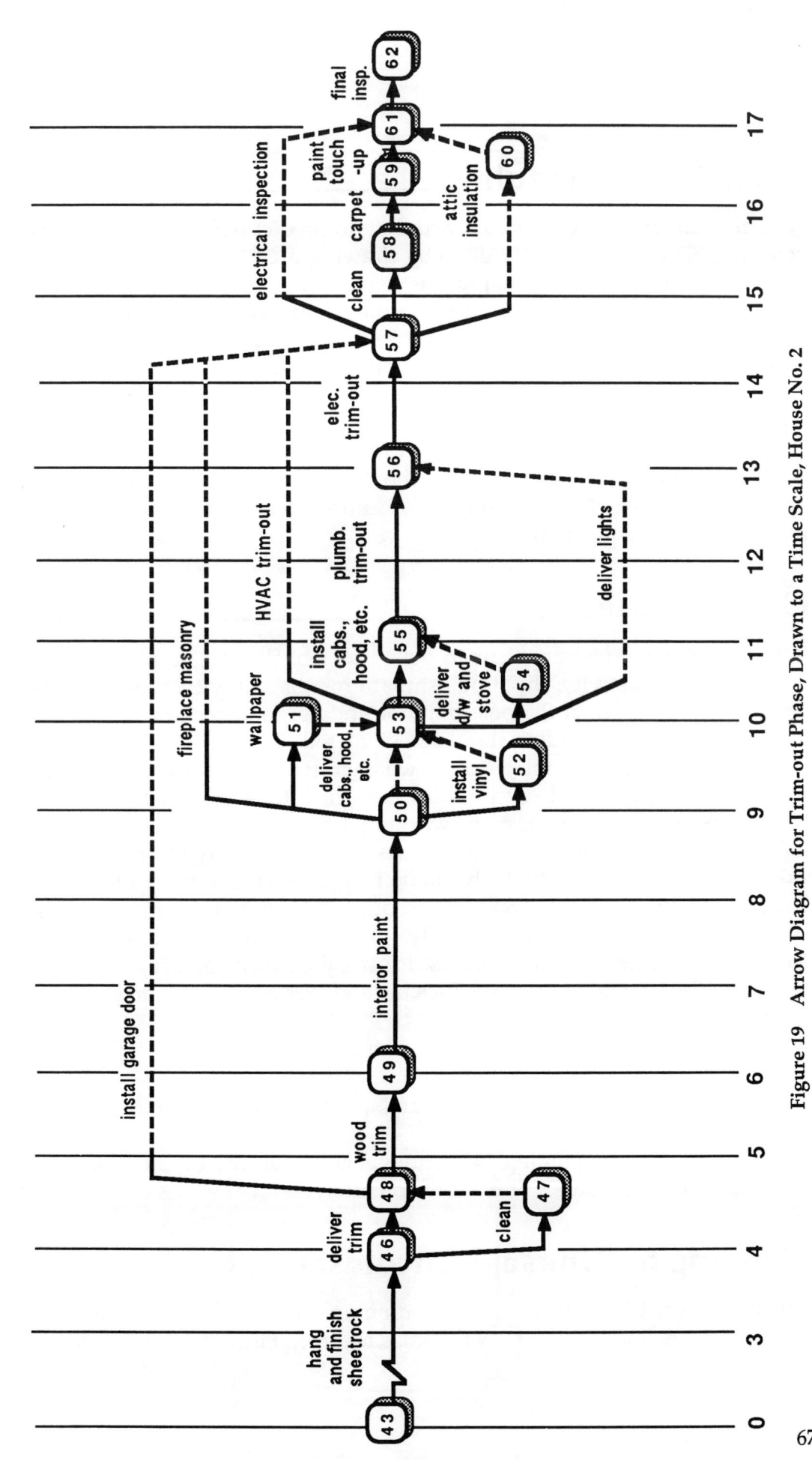

Long-Term Scheduling

A home builder uses long-term scheduling to predict when a house will be complete. This is most easily done by drawing a CPM diagram to a time scale on graph paper. The diagram is usually drawn using working days only and leaving out weekends and holidays. This will give the builder the total number of working days the project is scheduled to take. After the total number of working days is calculated, it is a simple matter to use a calendar to determine the completion date by leaving out weekends and holidays.

If the time seems too long or short to the builder based on experience with homes of similar size, he or she should reexamine each activity's time span. An as-built CPM diagram kept for future reference will eliminate this problem for subsequent houses.

Contingencies

Various contingencies can occur to delay the job. When a contingency involves just one activity, the time estimate for that activity should be increased. For example, if the possibility of underground rock could impede grading, the time for grading should be increased.

Some contingencies relate to the weather. Rain that could impede the work should be taken into account for the schedule. A common practice is to assume rain will fall at least one working day per week. For convenience, many schedulers assume rain on Wednesday. Any activity the rain would stop is left until Thursday, which could change the critical path. Of course, such a schedule does not mean that no outside work will ever be done on Wednesday. The schedule is simply including the possible effects of weather. If a certain Wednesday has dry weather, then the project gains a day. Likewise, should rain fall on Tuesday and Wednesday, the project loses a day.

In drier parts of the country, no outside work should be scheduled every other Wednesday. In wetter regions, a few more rain days should be put into the schedule. Cold weather can be handled similarly for jobs built in the winter.

The purpose of planning for contingencies is so the builder can estimate the completion date a little more accurately.

Planning for Unusual Circumstances

The nonstandard items that are specified on presold houses should be listed from the plans, specifications, or the sales contract. Since the local building and supply dealer will not automatically have every item, suppliers should be contacted to order these unusual items as soon as possible. The CPM diagram shows when the items will be needed, which can be compared to the expected delivery date from the supplier.

CHAPTER 4

The Monitoring Phase

The monitoring phase of the project is sometimes called the control phase. Here is where formal planning and scheduling techniques pay dividends.

Short-Term Control

The most effective use of CPM diagraming is to help with short-term control.

Weather forecasters can usually predict the weather for tomorrow. Their prediction for two days away is somewhat less reliable but usually fairly accurate. Five-day outlooks are common, but weather predictions five days away are not as accurate as predictions for tomorrow.

Scheduling a construction project is much the same. We can predict what will happen tomorrow with a fair degree of accuracy. Predicting what will happen five days away is a little less reliable. Bad weather, absentee subcontractors or workers, and material shortages all make accurate predictions difficult.

Many home builders don't try to look past tomorrow in their planning. However, builders who can predict their needs three, four, or even five days ahead with a fair degree of accuracy can be much more efficient in their managerial efforts. The proper use of the CPM diagram can make this happen.

On large commercial or industrial projects, periodic revisions to the CPM diagram reflect changed conditions and updated planning. Redrawing the diagram obviously takes a lot of time and is often impractical to the home builder whose needs can be adequately met in other ways.

The first step is to draw the diagram itself. It doesn't have to be to an exact time scale, but the more accurate it is, the better. Each diagram should clearly indicate which job it represents and then be put on the wall or somewhere convenient for quick reference.

As each activity is completed, the builder highlights the arrow with a colored pen or marker to show that the work has been done. In a similar way, the boxes of a precedence network may be lightly colored in. A percentage of the arrow or box is marked for activities of long durations as the work on them proceeds. By looking at the diagram, the builder can quickly see exactly where each project is and what has to be done next. Refer to the partial diagram shown in Figure 20.

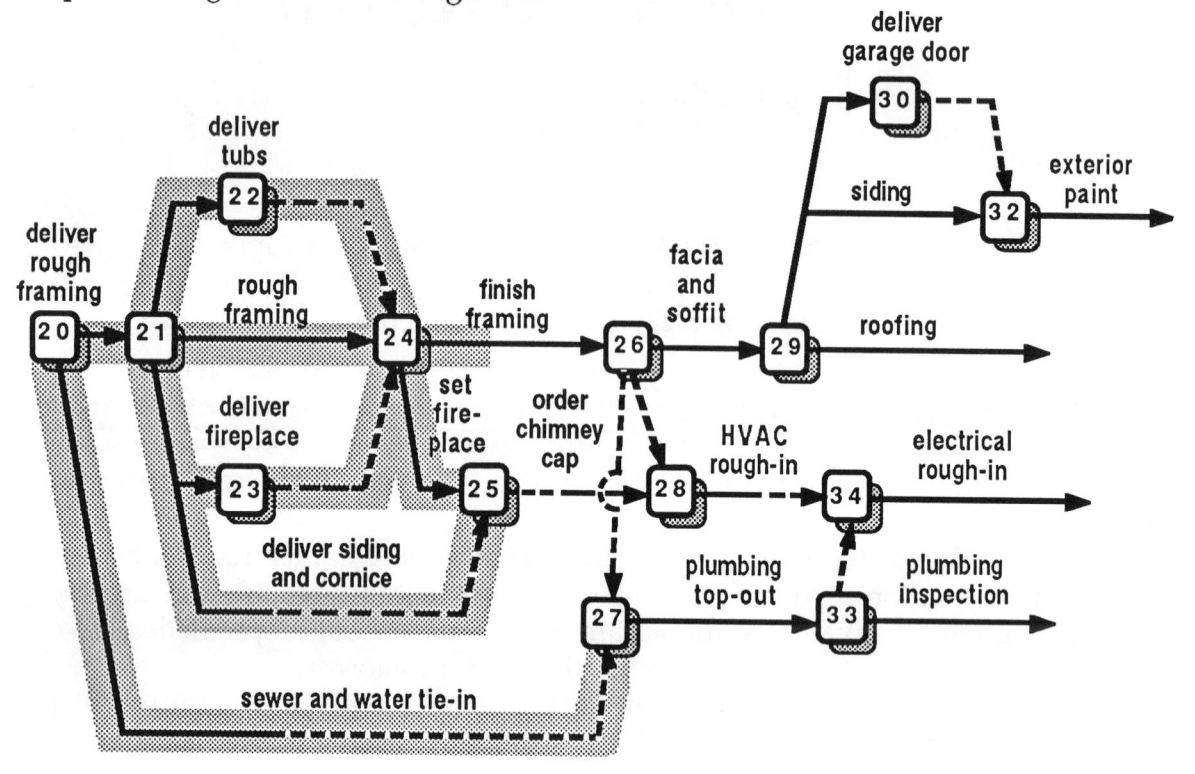

Figure 20 Using the Arrow Diagram for Short-Term Control

Assume that it is Monday morning. The carpenters have set the fireplace, which includes the siding around the chimney, are finishing the framing, and will be ready to start the facia and soffit by Tuesday afternoon. From the arrow diagram, the following actions can be taken:

1. The chimney can be measured and the cap ordered.
2. At the same time the cap is ordered, the heating and air conditioning subcontractor should be alerted to start Wednesday morning.
3. The plumber should be informed to start on Wednesday morning.
4. The plumber and the HVAC subcontractor have indicated that they will each take two days. Therefore, the electrician should be told to be ready to rough in the job on Friday and to expect a follow-up call to confirm.

72 Scheduling for Builders

5. The roofing can now be ordered and the roofer told to be ready by Friday.
6. The grading subcontractor should be told that the job will be ready for finish grading by Friday. This assumes that the plumbing inspector can do the inspection on Thursday.

If the builder follows this procedure daily, the work will flow more smoothly. Consequently, more work can be done in the same amount of time. Also, the builder will be following a cardinal rule of planning and scheduling—*make something happen every day on every job.*

Controlling Material Deliveries

Refer to the arrow diagram for House No. 1 shown in Figure 2. Notice that the brick is delivered after the lot is graded. The idea behind this is that the brick would get in the way if delivered before the grading. Likewise, the roof trusses are delivered one day before framing. Actually, these items may be ordered the first day of the job with instructions not to deliver until the days shown. Each builder must determine the long lead items based on suppliers and the operation.

Reminders to order those items may be noted on the CPM diagram with flags as shown in Figure 21.

Revising CPM Diagrams

Large commercial and industrial projects demand monthly updating of the CPM diagram because bad weather, material delays, and other unforeseeable factors can disrupt the original plan and schedule. Using the last diagram and job log, the contractor draws an as-built diagram for the past month, which brings the job up to date, and changes the future diagram to reflect the current state of the job. An out-of-date CPM diagram is worthless.

Some revisions involve changing the network logic to stay on schedule, for example, reevaluating soft constraints. The contractor may prefer to finish painting the exterior before doing the final cleanup and landscaping, but it doesn't have to be done this way. Rearranging the order of the activities is a common way for a builder to make up lost time.

Home builders rarely have to redraw a diagram to benefit from it throughout the job. Their diagrams are quite simple compared to those for large commercial or industrial projects. Also, if builders color in activities as completed, they can easily see where they are and what to do next. Usually minor logical changes can be handled without major redrawing efforts.

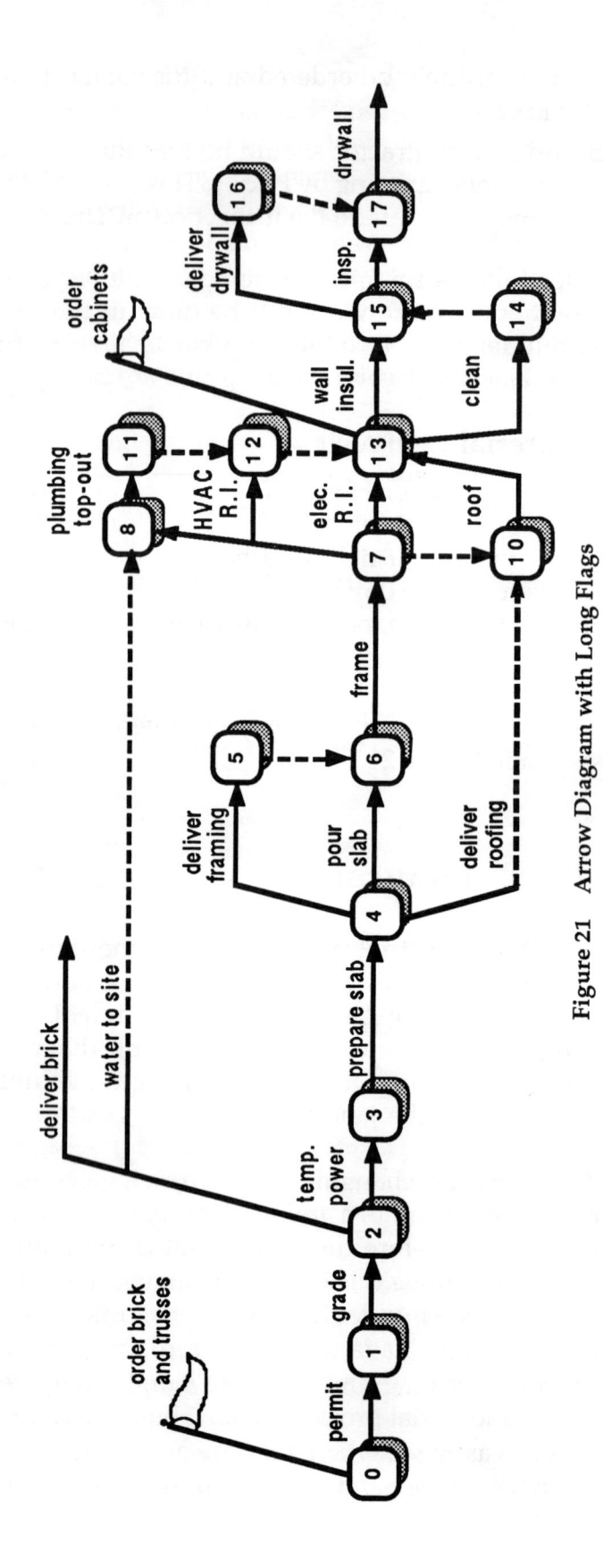

Figure 21 Arrow Diagram with Long Flags

74 Scheduling for Builders

Builders who plan in their heads have a general method in mind for a job. When unforeseen events force changes in the planned order of activities, these changes are done mentally. A diagram on paper can help the builder better organize thoughts when changes are necessary. For example, refer to Figure 7, the arrow diagram for the rough-in phase of House No. 2. Assume that the sewer tie-in cannot be made as planned for some reason. The diagram shows that the sewer tie-in should be done before the plumber comes back to top out the house. The plumbing top-out is a critical path item and any delay here will delay the whole job. Since sewer tie-in before plumbing top-out is a soft constraint, the plumber can top out the job and then come back later to do the tie-in.

Sometimes changing the order of activities might cost a little more. Suppose the garage door delivery is delayed for a few days. That might not affect the schedule because of the 11 float days in the path from garage door delivery through exterior paint and gutters to landscape. Assume now that the delay of the garage door is approaching 11 days, and if it doesn't come soon, the completion of the job will be delayed. If the house has already been sold, the builder stands to lose not only the daily cost of construction loan interest but also the buyer's goodwill. The painter can paint the rest of the house, which allows the gutters to be installed independently from the garage door. The landscaping can also proceed without the garage door. Even hanging the door unpainted after it finally arrives may be worth the cost of paying the painter to paint around the hardware just to get the job done on time.

The examples of changes in logic or the order of activities demonstrate that for simple diagrams redrawing is not always necessary. However, more complicated jobs with wholesale changes may be better served with a revised diagram.

Crashing a Project

If a job has fallen behind because of unexpected delays, the builder may have to take steps to finish the work sooner, otherwise known as crashing a job. There are two ways to crash a job.

First, the builder may put more people on the job, have subcontractors do the same, or work overtime. These actions may or may not cost extra. Inefficiencies and overtime rates should be weighed against losses caused by late completions. Since most builders subcontract the largest portion of their work, subcontractors depend upon builders for their livelihood. Most subcontractors will try to work with builders who need to crash or speed up a project as long as this only occurs occasionally.

Second, as mentioned earlier, the builder can change the order of activities by overlapping trades that normally would not work at the same time. The plumbing trim, electrical trim, HVAC trim, exterior paint, attic insulation, landscaping, and driveway may be done at the same time instead of how they are shown in Figure 2. Here again, this may or may not cost extra. A CPM diagram can often help a builder decide the best way to crash a job.

Cost Forecasting

Most jobs are financed in one of three ways:

- out of the builder's own funds
- by periodic payments from the owner of a presold house
- by funds borrowed from a bank or other lender

Furthermore, payments from the owner or lender may occur as needed, weekly, monthly, or at completion of the slab, rough-in, and trim-out phases of construction.

The ability to forecast cash needs helps builders who are financing jobs from their own funds. A builder may have a certificate of deposit where early withdrawal would result in a penalty or other similar time constraints on his or her money. It is fairly obvious that if builders could forecast cash needs, they could then make the best decisions about investments.

With a presold house, builders could enhance their image with the owner and thereby their reputation by giving the owner a projected cash requirement schedule. As many builders know, a good reputation is money in the bank.

Likewise, banks are favorably impressed with builders who conduct their business in a professional manner. Of course, builders who supply an owner or banker with a projected cash requirement schedule are under the gun, so to speak, to produce.

The ability to project cash flow is a real advantage when making draws at specific stages of completion. Usually material bills are due on the tenth of the month, and workers and subcontractors like to get paid on Friday. The following example gives the costs for House No. 1:

Activity	Subcontracted Labor	Materials
1. Get permit.	$ 100	$ 0
2. Grade lot.	800	0
3. Get temporary power.	30	0
4. Get water to site.	200	0
5. Deliver brick, etc.	0	2,100
6. Prepare slab.	1,700	650
7. Pour slab.	220	1,800
8. Deliver framing.	0	9,600
9. Frame.	1,650	0
10. Deliver roofing.	0	450
11. Put roofing on.	200	0
12. Rough in electrical work.	1,100	0
13. Rough in HVAC.	1,400	0
14. Top out plumbing.	1,100	0
15. Brick exterior.	1,400	0
16. Insulate walls.	400	0
17. Clean.	50	0
18. Inspect.	0	0
19. Hook up sewer.	350	0
20. Deliver drywall.	0	800
21. Hang and finish drywall.	700	0
22. Clean drywall scraps.	50	0
23. Put down vinyl.	220	1,200
24. Deliver trim.	0	1,500
25. Stain trim and paint.	1,100	0
26. Install cabinets.	200	2,000
27. Install wood trim.	900	0
28. Install ceramic tile.	300	0
29. Trim out plumbing.	1,000	0
30. Trim out electrical work.	900	0
31. Trim out HVAC.	750	0
32. Paint exterior.	850	0
33. Insulate attic.	550	0
34. Do final cleanup.	125	0
35. Landscape and pave drive.	1,800	0
36. Inspect.	0	0

These numbers may or may not reflect reality and are only given to demonstrate the procedure to forecast cash needs.

First, list all the activities on the arrow diagram. A dollar value is assigned to each activity for materials and subcontracted labor as shown. These numbers can be easily adapted from estimates.

The arrow diagram can be drawn to a time scale showing the days and a table drawn below the arrow diagram as shown in Figures 22a-b. The cost of each activity is then written in on the due date.

In this example, the permit is paid for when received, and the water and power deposits are paid for at the time of application. This particular example shows the job starting on the twelfth day of the month. Therefore, none of the material bills will come due until the tenth of the following month.

All subcontractors' bills are due on the Friday after they finish their work as shown on the table in Figure 22b. The complete total of projected cash expenditures for each day is also shown.

Now assume that the builder either owns the lot or has separate financing arrangements for the lot. And assume that the lender has agreed to lend $39,000 on the house—$13,000 at the completion of the slab phase, $13,000 at the completion of the rough-in phase, and $13,000 at final completion. The builder can make the first draw on September 21, the day the slab is poured. Between September 12 and September 21, the builder must spend $1,130 out of pocket ($100 + $230 + $800). On September 22, an additional $1,920 is due, leaving the builder $9,950 ahead ($13,000 - $3,050).

The second or rough-in draw can be made on September 29. By this time, the builder will have drawn $26,000 and spent $10,350 ($100 + $230 + $800 + $1,920 + $7,300).

At this point, the builder is $15,650 ahead ($26,000 - $10,350). On October 6, payments of $1,100 are made, leaving a positive balance of $14,550 ($15,650 - $1,100). On October 10, the material bills are due, leaving the builder $850 behind ($14,550 - $15,400). On October 13, another $2,420 must be paid out, which leaves the builder with a net $3,270 out of pocket (- $850 - $2,420).

On the following Friday, October 20, another $6,275 is payable, leaving the builder $9,545 out of pocket. The final inspection is on Monday after which the builder can draw the last $13,000 and use the balance toward the $4,700 due. Of course, the builder could crash the project by one day, move the final inspection to Friday, and save having to come up with the additional $6,275.

By using the procedure just described, the builder can determine the amount of out-of-pocket money required to pay bills as they come due during construction. The builder can quickly see how job size, schedule, and complexity will affect the amount of out-of-pocket money required. Being able to analyze these factors ahead of time gives the builder a certain amount of control so he or she can plan work more efficiently.

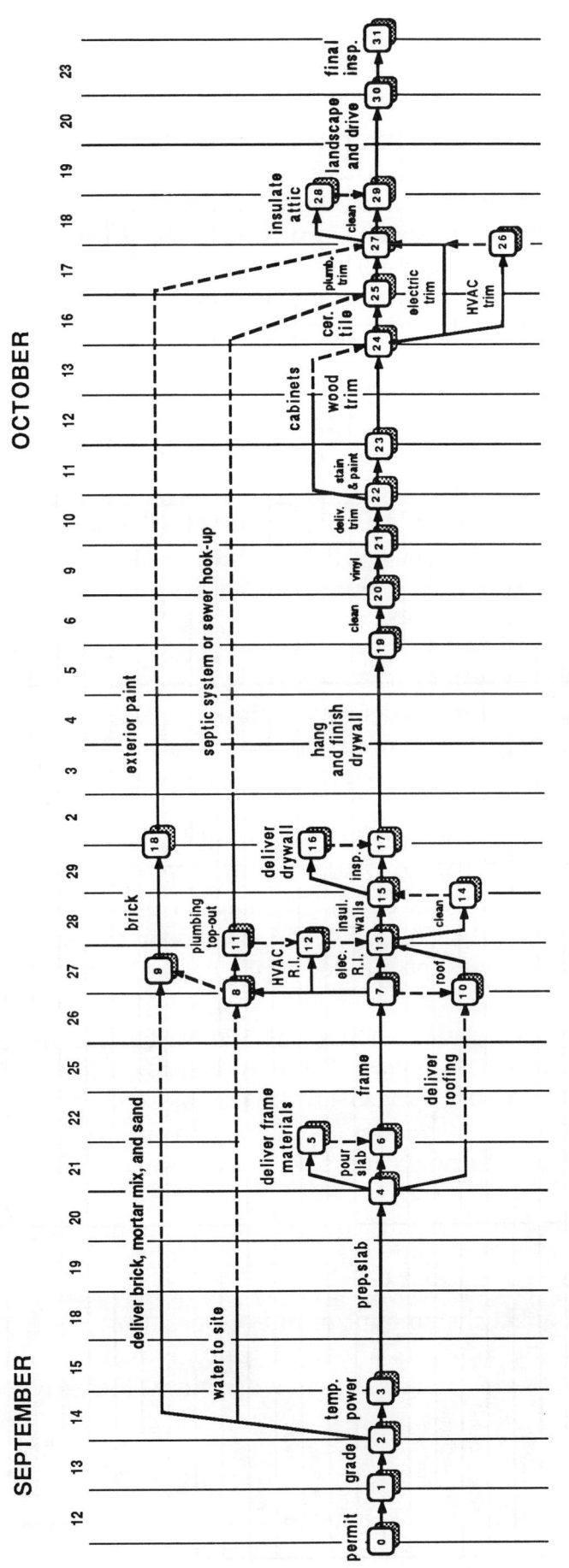

Figure 22a Cash Flow Forecast, House No. 1

SEPTEMBER / OCTOBER

	12	14	15	22	29	6	10	13	20	23
permit	100									
grade		230	800							
temporary power		30								
water to site		200								
deliver brick, etc.							2,100			
prepare slab				1,700			650			
pour slab				220			1,800			
deliver framing							9,600			
frame					1,650					
deliver roofing							450			
roof					200					
electrical rough-in					1,100					
HVAC rough-in					1,400					
plumbing top-out					1,100					
brick					1,400					
insulate walls					400					
clean					50					
sewer hook-up						350				
deliver drywall							800			
drywall						700				
clean						50				
vinyl								220		1,200
deliver trim										1,500
stain and paint								1,100		
cabinets								200		2,000
wood trim								900		
ceramic tile									300	
plumbing trim									1,000	
electric trim									900	
HVAC trim									750	
exterior paint									850	
insulate attic									550	
final clean									125	
landscape & drive									1,800	
Daily Total	100	230	800	1,920	7,300	1,100	15,400	2,420	6,275	4,700
Running Subtotal			1,130	3,050	10,350	11,450	29,270		35,545	40,245

Figure 22b Cash Flow Forecast, House No. 1

Legal Implications

A CPM diagram is just a plan showing the order and the time in which the builder plans to do the various activities of a job. In the event of a dispute about time, such as finishing a job late or not being ready for a subcontractor as originally planned, the CPM diagram could be used against the builder in a court proceeding under the theory that the CPM diagram represents a commitment on the part of the builder to do various segments of the work by certain times. The chance of this happening is rare, but such actions have been brought. Therefore, the builder should take steps for his or her protection in the case of a dispute. The first thing is not to give out copies of CPM diagrams indiscriminately. If it is necessary to hand out a CPM diagram, add a note that the diagram is simply a planning guide for the sole use of the builder and should not be interpreted as a commitment to do anything other than what is in the contract.

Multiproject Scheduling

If a builder has several projects going at the same time, CPM diagrams can plan the use of labor or subcontractors. By using diagrams to a time scale, the builder can see possible conflicts early, such as the framers being needed on two jobs at the same time. The earlier the conflict can be seen, the easier it is to make adjustments. The builder can use many refinements to plan work for simultaneous projects. One method is to draw a CPM diagram for one job and then to draw succeeding jobs farther down the same page. Another method is to draw the CPM diagram for each job to a time scale on separate pieces of paper and then line the diagrams up to pick out possible conflicts.

Ideally the crews will finish their assigned tasks and then move on to the next house following the preceding crews who have just finished and moved on. Say, for example, that a builder has several houses under construction at the same time. It might be possible under some circumstances to go to the last house and see the grading operation, to the house before that and see the slab being put in, and to the house before that and see the framing.

Since the framing activities require more time than any other craft, this particular trade will control the scheduling of multiple projects. If only one framing crew is used and seven days are spent framing each house, the builder will be limited to a maximum of 36 houses per year, assuming no days lost due to bad weather. Given five holidays, there are 255 work days per year, which when divided by seven days per house give 36 houses when working every day. For this to work out, the builder must stagger the jobs such that when the carpenters are finished with one house, another slab or foundation is ready.

If the builder wants to build more houses and is constrained by the framing activities, the only solution is to add more carpenters. If crew sizes are simply increased, a proportional reduction in time may not result. As in most construction activities, framing has an optimum crew size and increases in carpenters beyond that size result in inefficiencies. Therefore, the prudent thing to do is either to have two or more framing crews working on different houses or to split the work and let one crew do the rough and finish carpentry and another crew do the facia, soffit, and siding. If this action is taken, the painting, which takes five days—two for the exterior and three for the interior, will become the controlling craft. Unlike carpentry, painting is an activity for which an increase in crew size up to a point will not cause a noticeable loss of efficiency.

So, in multiproject scheduling, the use of CPM diagraming can help not only to coordinate the movement of crews from house to house but also to coordinate the division of work, number of crews, and crew sizes.

The CPM diagram can be used as a general planning tool for multiproject scheduling. As an example, assume that a builder is building homes similar to House No. 2. The arrow diagrams for this house in Figures 17, 18, and 19 show that the framing carpenter will average spending seven days on each job—two days to rough frame, two days to finish frame, one day on facia and soffit, and two days on siding. Many builders also have their framing carpenter do other activities, such as locate the house site, lay out the footings, set the batter boards, and form the garage slab. But these are activities of short duration, each taking only a half day or less, and do not require more than two people. If these activities do not substantially subtract from the crew's performance or are done by others, it is safe to assume that the framing carpenters are tied up for an average of seven days per house.

Summary

Formal planning and scheduling can be done on any level. Almost any builder can benefit by using these procedures at a level that best suits his or her needs. Even a list of activities may be useful. For most people who do not use any written planning methods, a simple arrow diagram without units of time can be a big help.

Many builders knowledgeable about CPM diagraming draw their diagrams to a time scale and mark off activities with a colored marker to keep track of the job.

For those willing to learn to draw and use a CPM diagram, their work will almost certainly become easier.